The Success Attitude

Haunting Messages Guiding Us

Janice Davies

1st WORLD
PUBLISHING

The Success Attitude

Haunting Messages Guiding Us

Janice Davies

Copyright © Janice Davies 2011

Published by 1stWorld Publishing
P.O. Box 2211, Fairfield, Iowa 52556
tel: 641-209-5000 • fax: 866-440-5234
web: www.1stworldpublishing.com

First Edition

LCCN: 2011941236
SoftCover ISBN: 978-1-4218-8631-2
HardCover ISBN: 978-1-4218-8632-9
eBook ISBN: 978-1-4218-8633-6

This material has been written and published for educational purposes to enhance one's wellbeing. In regard to health issues, the information is not intended as a substitute for appropriate care and advice from health professionals, nor does it equate to the assumption of medical or any other form of liability on the part of the publisher or author. The publisher and author shall have neither liability nor responsibility to any person or entity with respect to loss, damages or injury claimed to be caused directly or indirectly by any information in this book.

To my beautiful daughters. . . my biggest pleasure and learning curve who provided me with an added incentive to be a positive role model as their mother.

Janice Davies - the lady with nice in her name
9/8/1954 – Life Purpose = Humanitarian

Praise for *The Success Attitude*

I found Janice's book to be thought provoking and wanted to know more. The exercises at the end of each chapter are great, they help to summarize the information, then ask you to focus on the direction your life has taken and give you an opportunity to change that direction if you choose to. This is another very valuable tool to help you on your journey.

—Trish Stewart Wholistic Harmony

The Success Attitude – Haunting Messages Guiding Us is the amazing story of Janice's journey of dealing with experiences from beyond. Over the years I've known her, she has shared her many experiences with me and the courage she has shown when being faced with these encounters. This is a very special read for anyone who has had similar experiences and has been confused by them. It is my belief that such visits are designed for us mere mortals to understand and tap into our highest good.

—Ann Andrews – The Corporate Tool Box & Teams Woe to Go

I have had the pleasure of reading Janice's book and loved it. Janice's experiences in life are easily related to and written in a humourous and enlightening way. I enjoy the way Janice embraces thinking 'outside the square'. A great read.

—Kaylene Lawry-Smith – The Travelling Companion

Over the years I have known Janice, as a dear friend and fellow traveler on this road we call life. Along her many paths in life she been lead by an inner voice that has challenged and encouraged her to accept the invisible and unknown aspects of life while coming to understand that these experiences are so often more profound in truth than the seeing eye can perceive.

Janice has always shown a capacity to keep stepping out of her comfort zone to embrace new horizons of self learning and discovery while also following her inner guidance to work in ways to help others to discover their own self worth and purpose in life.

Janice has written her book with a deep and genuine desire to share her experiences in order to encourage other people to share their own special story with more confidence of being heard and accepted.

—Rev. Rhonda joy Gola Unity Minister.

Contents

Acknowledgements

I'd like to acknowledge my Mother and Father, whose love supported me through all the ups and downs in my life. Without them, my journey would have been much harder and very different. Also thanks to my siblings and their partners.

Thanks to my mentor Ann Andrews, Leigh Kelly who introduced new dimensions into my life, Reverend Rhonda Gola for her spiritual wisdom and support, Kaylene Lawry-Smith who always had a smile when needed and both her and Trish Stewart who helped oversee my final copy.

I'd like to acknowledge Kerry my partner who has provided another journey where I am always learning to become my best, whilst creating my heaven on earth.

These words are aligned to a

Higher Consciousness to

Universal laws and

Mankind . . .

Far greater than

the Physical ME.

Janice May Davies
The lady with nice in her name
Attitude Specialist

Sailors and Onion Skins

You can't change the direction of the wind
But you can change the sails.

—Unknown

Some people believe we chose our destiny before birth. Others discredit that theory. Many have 'celestial,' 'super-human' or 'spiritual' experiences that change the course of their lives. A few are earth shattering, others are quiet and subtle. A number are mystical and ancient dating back thousands of years. Some folk believe in different Gods; Buddha, Sai Baba and an array of others. To me, it does not matter as long as their message is about 'unconditional love' and that it supports mankind.

Then, some probably like me are puzzled by our experiences. We question and search for understanding, only to go in circles until we answer the plea or call to take action and 'feel' on track with our lives.

I have never seen my life as interesting compared to others. I have not climbed mountains, won races, sailed the seven seas or been a wonder cook.

However, I have learned that others recognize abilities in us that we don't see ourselves and that events happen in life without our being able to comprehend them.

The famous quote, *"When the student is ready, the teacher appears,"* explains this journey. Albeit unknown to me as the student I must have been ready. The teacher, 'the universe,' has taught me about our internal power on our personal journey to success. Now, by reading this book, you and others in the world may be the next students ready to learn.

Unknown to me at the time, I have been blessed as one of the chosen, destined to walk an enlightened path. Subsequently, I have encountered a few extra-ordinary experiences sent to me so I could learn. Like the explorers who sailed across the seas when they were convinced the earth was not flat, propelled by nothing but a gut feeling, courage and a dream, they leap frogged their exploration and discoveries into the history books and changed the world.

There are many things I do not know in life. However, I do know that as bizarre as it seems, the universe is urging me forward to learn more. This is a challenging task and has me stepping out in faith as I learn another life lesson.

The worlds' movers and shakers like Oprah, Nelson Mandela, Gandhi, Mother Theresa and thousands of others, have all overcome challenges to follow their life purpose in order to help others and make a difference. Interestingly, Susan Boyle, our latest hero who has taken the world by storm, had the same challenges with self-esteem and bullying that I'd had at school. Peeling back the skin of an onion reveals a vegetable useful in many different dishes to millions of chefs around the world. Peeling back the hardened outer facade of a person reveals a soft heart and soul that can resonate something more useful to mankind.

As individuals, we are unique and are born to embrace our inner self. Each of us is imbedded with free will to develop ourselves and create our personal journey of fulfillment, happiness and success in the world. The journey is never smooth running, yet the hurdles are where our life lessons lie and only strengthen us. Nelson Mandela said that "our personal power is in our ability to like ourselves." Many other artists have expressed this to the world through song as well:

> Frank Sinatra – *My Way*
>
> M People – *Search for the Hero*
>
> Whitney Houston – *The Greatest Love of All*
>
> Robbie Williams – *Angels*

I did not fully understand the significance of my journey until recently, and only after I had learned many lessons about life. Now, with passionate enthusiasm, I am working towards a new journey as I share it with the world and try to make a difference. The words in this book might resonate with something within yourself, or maybe there is someone else you know who would benefit from this empowering message. In essence, as I have been 'shoulder tapped' to make a difference, by you reading this book, have now been shoulder tapped to make a difference as well.

That is the secret behind *The Success Attitude - Haunting Messages Guiding Us*. I needed to understand the significance and embrace my role in them. I have had to move forward in faith, allowing comprehension to evolve before I came to this verdict:

> *Everyone in the world is supported both*
> *physically and spiritually as we*
> *overcome our personal hurdles to embrace the*
> *positive and live our destined life.*
>
> —Janice

Many people are happy with spirituality in religion. I am suggesting the other less conventional 'spirit' encounters as well. There will always be the hurdles and negativity from others and in our thoughts. We have free will to master both experiences from both the physical and spirit worlds to direct us. I suggest you always focus on the positive . . . and learn to overcome negativity and only then will you find success and happiness across all areas of your life.

Then, like the early explorers, we need to follow our intuition and gut feelings and find the courage and wisdom to follow our inner compass on our individual journey to help first ourselves, and then mankind.

Now my story begins . . .

Chapter 1

The Swan, Adventurer and Leader

What lies behind us and what lies before us,
are tiny matters to what lies within us.

—Ralph Waldo Emerson

One blissful childhood experience of mine was in 1959, of me sitting in the big white swan of the kindergarten class parade float. The head of the swan stood nearly twenty feet off the ground and it had thousands of squares of white crepe paper pushed into the wire netting to resemble feathers. In the middle of its wide back was a hole where I sat in my yellow shirred dress and my big matching yellow bonnet. I was waving to the local town crowd celebrating the opening of the bridge in Huntly. At four years old, I seemed comfortable being the center of attention and maybe that was an omen for the future. The ugly duckling turning into a beautiful white swan!

Not that I recall being ugly, except in baby photos when I had a bump on my head. Maybe it was from my bottle getting dropped back into the stroller, after I was being teased. I cannot remember it happening, but it's a good story.

Born the middle daughter of a family with three girls and one boy, I was a tomboy, but obviously had to wear dresses due to my mother's insistence. Throughout my life I was never in the 'popular' group as I was always on a different path. I always appeared one step off to the side of the crowd, pushing different boundaries of my own.

Over the years when I have spoken to people about their childhood, it appears they did not have anything like mine. And in fact, as a child I was very lucky to have had such wonderful parents who taught us how to enjoy life and have adventures. Some theorize that we chose our parents before we are born, although I haven't fully investigated that theory, it is an interesting concept. Though if that is true, I made a good choice of parents.

Looking back in the family photos, my parents had been campers from the early days before we were even a twinkle in their eyes. They continued that tradition on throughout their lives and shared it with others in the many community groups they joined.

As kids, preparing for our annual six-week vacation to Maraetai camping ground was a mission. We had a large family tent and many 'extras' to gather. The trailer dad had converted into an A frame bed-room with collapsible beds and a canvas roof. It became an outside bedroom for us girls and my brother was in a pup tent. A trestle table was always placed at the front of the main tent, the congregation place for meals, social times and the cards games during the evening.

Preparing each year undoubtedly was a marathon for Mum. Over the years the amount of stuff we took grew, and Mum always said, "Morris refused to take the kitchen sink." To add to the organized chaos of preparation, on Christmas Eve the plums were always ripe and home-made jam was cooked. This was a family tradition I was to continue before my big adventure in years to come.

We camped with our cousins, spending countless days on the beach, swimming, fishing, sailing and even attending Sunday School on the beach. We continued this traditional meet up every year until I was ten, when the camping ground was closed and turned into a car park and it was time for change.

During the last years of camping Dad and a group of other fathers had built a small fleet of 'P Class' yachts. They loved sailing and passed that love onto to their families. Every Sunday afternoon we sailed on Hakanoa Lake in Huntly. On the long weekends the four families would embark on adventures to Rotorua or Thames for the yachting regattas. We had a great time and would always explore the tourist spots, countryside and beaches.

After the Maraetai campground closed, it ended our camping. Mum wanted a bit more comfort. Dad was a do-it-yourself man, and so on the back of a cereal box he designed our first caravan. The measurements were simple; the door had to be as wide as Mum's hips (which weren't too wide), and the yacht had to fit in the middle of the caravan for transport to the yachting regattas.

Over the winter months, when the caravan was being built, one of my jobs was to help my father rivet together the aluminum as it lay on the garage floor. As a tomboy, I enjoyed the task immensely, and forty years later I still own my hammer. I've passed this skill to my daughters who can use the electric drill and are into DIY projects as well.

Once finished building the caravan, our Christmas vacations for the next few years were spent traveling around the North Island. At each of the camping grounds a flag was purchased to hang on the curtain wire in the back window.

Our virgin adventure was down via Rotorua to the East Coast, Gisborne and Lake Waikaremoana. Our first camping ground was in the Blue Lakes in Rotorua. We had been told to pack light with not too many clothes—which we all did. However, we hadn't been prepared for the freezing temperature on the first night, and had even pulled the floor mats up on top of the blankets to keep us warm in bed. Needless to say, the next day we went shopping for warmer clothes.

The road into Lake Waikaremoana was narrow and scary. It wound around the hills and valleys, hugging the mountains. Looking down at the huge drop to the bottom of the gorge, I recall thinking, "that would be a long way to fall." The lake was magnificent. Little did I realize that twenty-five years later I would revisit the lake to tramp the tracks on its shores with a business group and create new dreams.

After a few years of traveling around the North Island, my parents fell in love with Martins Bay and we continued the vacation tradition in that campsite. Years had passed and the entourage now included a fizz boat, extra childhood friends, cars, water-skis and other important gear like the smoker for captured fish.

Eventually, a section was purchased at a nearby beach. Family and friends traveled there for our boating and Christmas vacations, a tradition that still continues to this day.

As youngsters we took these holidays for granted, whereas while there was never a lot of money, we were fortunate to have experienced such a wonderful childhood. These memories live forever as highlights in our lives and experiences that make us happy.

In today's society where people think money dictates happiness, we need to recall that nature provides us with ample opportunities to enjoy and experience life. A stroll on the beach and a paddle in the sea is always good for the soul and clears our mind to ideas for our future.

In one of the many personal development workshops I have attended, one exercise we completed was to create a time line of the high and low points of our life. I still use this with clients today to decide which points made them happy and wish to repeat and which low points to avoid.

One of my memorable highlights recollects primary school. My teacher always looked very serious with her hair pulled back in a bun, long skirts and collar buttoned to her neck. We stood in two lines outside our classroom ready to enter the class after lunch.

"Only one person has achieved one hundred percent in the spelling test," she announced in a very stern voice. "Only one person had put the silent 'n' on the word autumn."

Maybe she was disappointed more of her pupils didn't get the spelling test correct, I'm not sure. I listened with in trepidation. I had worked hard learning the words for the spelling test the night before.

The teacher looked around the room. "The one student is . . . Janice Davies."

As my name was called out, the others looked at me. I was so proud and am sure I puffed out my chest (before I had one to impress the opposite sex with), and rose up in height and blossomed for a moment. That one moment of triumph has stayed with me for life. I liked being a winner!

In hindsight, my school days were great. I didn't think that then, of course, as many of us don't. However, as children they were the most carefree times of our lives before our chaotic teenage years and adulthood responsibility.

Other talents were added to my spelling skills at school. Peeling the potatoes and orientation skills at school camps as well as earning badges for floristry and knots during my years at Girls Brigade (similar to Girl Scouts) rounded out my list of achievements. Saturday mornings were spent playing tennis, Tuesday nights tapping my toes at Scottish dancing—though I was never able to master the 'fancy tricky' dances. Albeit, somehow, someone during the first ten years of my life, glimpsed in me leadership skills I was unaware I possessed. As a result, at Huntly Primary School I was made head girl prefect (also known as the school president).

The school motto was 'Knowledge is Power.' Now in my fifties I realize that I have lived the past twenty-five years by that motto. I had a gap in time when I became sidetracked into a negative low point. My analysis of myself as 'slow learner and a late developer' explains a period in life when I was 'lost and unhappy,' though I was unaware of it at the time.

> *"There are known knowns. These are things we know that we know. There are known unknowns. That is to say, there are things that we now know we don't know. But there are also unknown unknowns. There are things we do not know we don't know."*

Ghandi refers to his life as, *"My life is my teaching which is my story,"* and I would like to embrace his concept as well.

Being head prefect held some responsibility. I ran prefect meetings and spoke at the school assemblies. I still have my prefect badge to-day, as a memento from the past. In hindsight this was my early training, which is the underlying experiences from childhood preparing us for life.

When we weren't playing tennis we went through a stage of cleaning the church on Saturday mornings. Obviously my mother thought we should get on the good side of the man above. My sisters and I quickly tried to create some fun. If we dusted quickly, we were rewarded with a few moments standing in the ministers' pulpit, giving our imaginary sermons, waiting for Mum to finish. And, although we had piano lessons and played at home, we were never allowed to pump out our songs on the church organ. Not for one moment did I ever think these antics might pave my future path.

As I developed physically through my preteen years, naturally members of the opposite sex became of interest to me. There was no true heartthrob nor did I have lanky lads after me either. Most of the boys were my brother's friends and became like brothers to me.

However, there was one boy that caught my eye—I'm not sure if it was his hair, cute face or the fact he was somewhat "forbidden territory,"—definitely not who my parents would have wished for me to date.

This particular boy was from the wrong side of town, and there are plenty of stories about those types of relationships. However, the biggest challenge beyond my parents not liking him was the fact that a group of girls also from the other side of town did not like me either.

Their threats and behavior eventually bullied me into fogginess. They would get into groups of three or four and follow me around the high school and make comments that they were going to "beat me up."

Thus, to avoid any more attention, I chose instead not to seek the limelight of parades, leadership and achieving, but instead to fade and hide in the background to avoid their taunting.

During those few years of my youth I eventually lost my confidence and belief in myself. Unbeknown to me, instead of continuing on my life as a leader and rising to the occasion, I said probably the first, worst, and most important 'no' in my life.

Why do I recall it? Well, once again, the old adage that others see skills in you which you do not see yourself rings very true. I was asked to be a high school prefect for the second time in my life. However, instead of saying 'yes' to my growth and journey of life of learning to become the best I could, and although it may have been the first word that entered my thoughts, instead out of my mouth came the word, "no."

I turned down the offer to stand out and be noticed in the crowd. I felt intimidated and bullied by this group of girls. I wanted to fade into my surroundings. I refused to be the leader that others wanted me to be. I recall a teacher pulling me aside and asking me why I did not want to take on the role. My reply was simply, "I just don't want to." How do you say you are scared of being thumped?

It would have been a great opportunity for me. The prefects had their own room and I would be in a role that used my natural talent.

But instead I turned down the invitation to be a prefect, because I could hide. If I had said 'yes' this story would be very different.

It would not be until almost two decades later, that I started to say 'yes' again.

In my motivational presentations, which I have improved on after standing at the pulpit after cleaning the church and school assemblies, I count it as eighteen years, nine months, eight days, seven hours, six minutes and five seconds, because it is an easy countdown to remember.

Hindsight Insight

When you are children you have the chance to be your 'natural self.' We have the opportunity to play with 'what we love' and usually we play with that activity the most. It may be reading, making Lego constructions, dressing up, puzzles, organizing people, playing sports or making sandcastles. Those moments are guides to your natural gifts and even personality.

If you are searching for yourself, think back to your childhood for direction. What can you discover you have left behind?

_____

_____

_____

_____

_____

_____

Critical turning points are events in our life that inspire us further or draw us back into ourselves. They are moments in time when we make major decisions that alter our life and thoughts. When I completed my time line, being the winner of the spelling test was a high point and the bullying was a low point. Once I understood this I knew what future experiences would benefit me and what to avoid.

What critical turning points have you experienced that you do not want to re-create or happy experiences that you wish to repeat?

_____

_____

_____

_____

_____

_____

Chapter 2

The Third Semester

Success comes in cans, not cannots.

—Joel Weldon

At an early age, my sisters and brother all started to learn the piano. Over the years, we were driven to our lessons at seven o'clock each morning for thirty minute sessions. This continued for years although I never mastered the classical music. It was a family tradition to learn to play "Rembrance," and later "The Entertainer" by Scott Joplin. Making the excuse to practice piano was a great way to get out of jobs for awhile, although once we had a television we couldn't practice at night as they were both in our lounge room.

Dad was Welsh and loved to sing and played the mouth organ. In his younger days he had enjoyed family sing-a-longs around the piano and once we had our own piano, he taught himself to play. He couldn't read music so gradually we learned to play the songs he loved by his example. It became another family tradition to have a 'sing song' around the piano with his favourite songs like "Bye, Bye Black-bird," "The White Cliffs of Dover," and many more. Social times with friends and family also included these with Dad on the mouth organ and everyone gathered around singing and dancing.

In our teenage years it is a normal part of human development to start to push boundaries and exert ourselves. I had learned this during my play center and human development courses years later, and it happens in the third seven-year phase of our life. Up until then, I was a go with the flow sort of girl, but I was quickly learning to express myself. My family was visiting my grandmother in the hospital who I had visited a few times. I hated it and refused to go and my excuse was that I had piano practice. As the rest of the family left, the melodies of "Rembrance" billowed from the piano as I waved them good-by. That was a 'no' I remembered saying.

And this is another one: During my high school years I had been offered drugs and refused. Consequently, I thought at least I was reasonably sensible. I was never sure whether it was because I might like them or because I thought I am silly enough without them.

Unfortunately, I was not a scholar either. In high school it was School Certificate exams in my third year. I struggled with math but loved bookkeeping and geography and was mediocre at English. We had a *hand-me-to parent's* dog, inherited from my sister who kept me company during my school years. Henry was a black and white blue merle and sat through my nights of studying in my downstairs bedroom. In fact, he sat in front of the heater with other family members exams, in the same room, so may have been the most intelligent dog globally. Maybe the others did not vocalize as they studied as I did. Anyway, I managed to pass five school certificate topics . . . squeezing through with fifty-one percent for math. That was the highlight of my academic career.

In the following year, I changed math for art history, which was a very different topic. I don't know why I was interested in this—no-one I knew was interested in art history, so all I can say was that it tickled my fancy. Some theorize that if we have a past life, we have interests from our past that we bring into our present life. I'm not sure about the accuracy of that theory, but it is interesting mindset. When I was eligible to get into University Entrance in the 1970's I failed by four marks. So, becoming a 'wise and analytical person' was never on my agenda.

After leaving Huntly College, I started the first of my real careers. My interest as a dress designer had begun at the age of twelve. My nana gave me my first piece of green striped and paisley material and I sewed my first dress. It was a shift with a frill around the bottom. It was sewn on my antique Treadle Singer sewing machine which was brought for 2/6pence from a Rotary stall.

In high school, I was a follower of fashion magazines and designed my own clothes. In Huntly I was cutting edge in the fashion scene.

I wore bright blue turquoise satin hot pants with a long white lace overcoat to a school dance. I probably got a few glances.

Another of my outfits was a maroon pant set. It consisted of bell-bottom hipster trousers with 'oh so modern' buttons down the front instead of a zipper. I also had a long, sleeveless polyester coat, which was the latest trendy fabric. I must have been a real trend setter at our social events.

That was the era of Woodstock, when free love hit the world. Not that I indulged! My closest experience was at weekend music festivals camping out in the adjoining town of Ngaruawahia. We took pup tents, sleeping bags and Henry, and had a weekend of fun. Hundreds flocked to the paddocks on a local farm to listen to the bands play their music. It was New Zealand's answer to Woodstock, now replaced by the Big Day Out, Parachute and other concerts.

My tertiary training was completed by attending the New Zealand College of Fashion Design in Karangahape Road, Auckland. Previously I had altered patterns to create my masterpieces which in comparison was rather 'slap dash.' There I learned the tools of the trade as a fashion designer. Everything had a proper pattern, was fitted and tailored properly, which was a good lesson for me. I traveled from Huntly to Auckland every week and boarded with my aunty. On Friday night I traveled back to the social scene of Huntly. Our closest nightclub was in Hamilton twenty miles away where I wore some of my snazzy fashion items.

One night, when I was the only female in the group, the boys gave me a small bottle of rum to hide in my handbag. In the 1970's alcohol was not served in the nightclubs so we were breaking the law, slipping a drop or two into our glasses of Coca Cola. We had been told there had been an occasional raid by the police for alcohol. Murphy's Law came true—as there was one that night! The police searched my handbag and my brother admitted it was his. We were issued with a court order and suggestion to tell our parents as soon as possible. We decided it was better to tell them immediately, rather than receiving a telephone call or visit from the police on Sunday morning. Consequently, at three o'clock that morning we woke our parents and told them about our incident.

I was studying in Auckland when our court appearance occurred. My older sister, who was the academic of the family, wrote my letter for presentation in the court. I cannot recall the exact outcome, but it was probably nothing more than a rap over our knuckles.

My first job after Design College was managing a maternity boutique and finishing the clothes in Takapuna. I always laugh when I remember my time there. I was eighteen years old and pregnant ladies asked me about 'putting on weight' and would their arms get fat as well as their stomachs. I had no idea!

My pay was meager, but the owners must have thought that I was not experienced or maybe not confident enough to stand up for myself, I'm not sure which. Finally, I did ask for a pay rise and their answer was no. In that moment, I decided I WAS worth more, and handed in my notice. Shocked by my decision, they offered me a wage increase a few days later, but by that time I had chosen another goal for my life and declined. Not long after I left, the boutique closed.

My goal was my first overseas trip to Australia. I stayed with my cousins who were oyster farmers, near Newcastle in New South Wales. I worked in a local supermarket at the checkout in the sleepy seaside village of Port Stephens. The pay was low, but it was work. Eventually I left because I twisted my back carrying groceries from the customers' trolley. I was given a job by a cousin's friend and starting traveling in Newcastle. After six months I returned to New Zealand.

I had been invited to travel overseas to London with a friend from college with her two friends, and my answer was a resounding yes! Adventure, excitement and new places enticed me. So it was back to my hometown to start saving my dollars.

My parents welcomed me home. I worked in my father's office during the day and then walked one hundred meters up the road to start my second job of cleaning the Bendon factory. It was dusty as I swept around the hundreds of machines that churned out ladies underwear. I finished by eight o'clock and then it was home for tea.

I don't recall paying much rent . . . in fact probably didn't at home and again socialized with my big brother and his friends over the next few years, preparing for my big overseas experience.

Huntly was a small town, and traveling for the younger generation was just becoming possible, affordable and slightly trendy. Only one other guy I knew had travelled to London from Huntly, so in fact, thinking back, I was a bit of a trendsetter in that area as well, this time not with clothes . . . but still adventurous as I embarked on my journey to the other side of the world.

My twenty-first birthday was on August 9, 1975. It was a fancy dress party and a great social event with fifty or sixty people. I have since heard that our friends knew they could always count on a great party happening at the Davies' household. Years later I found the answer to be the rapid growth and plentiful fruit on the lemon and grapefruit trees. It was the outside toilet for the men! I might not have enjoyed the fruit so much if I had known!

My girl friends and I had decided to wait until after that party, before embarking on our adventure to London, because that's when the air-fares were cheaper in the low season.

Four days later, we were on the plane!

Hindsight Insight

Utilizing your natural gifts, talents and your personality traits can guide you to your true potential. One of mine was that I was creative person. When you are an adult searching for happiness, you can delve back into your younger years and search out your passions from childhood. Additionally, as parents you can guide your children into careers by taking from their childhood passions.

What can you rediscover about your passions? Are you including them in some form in your life?

_____

_____

_____

_____

_____

_____

When you find goals you are passionate about, you become committed. In essence, it is your head following your heart and soul. Life is about creating happiness from your insides and expressing this outwards. You find your passion and then your thoughts need to create goals to achieve it. Often people live in reverse, thinking or being told you should love certain things, so that you should have these goals.

Which method do you use for your goals? What do you need to change?

_____

_____

_____

_____

_____

_____

Chapter 3
Adventuring

Challenges can be stepping stones or stumbling blocks.
It's just a matter of how you view them.

—Anon

Living and working in Henry VIII's Hunting Lodge in Thames Ditton was an exciting entrance into the history of England. The Fourteenth Century building was the classic old English-style building with white walls, wooden battens at the windows, red velvet seats, fireplaces, low ceilings and full of hunting pictures on the wall with an ambience of old world charm.

When I looked along the length of the upstairs hallway, the ceiling was crooked and the floor dipped down. I never knew if the lodge was haunted, but I wondered who walked along these corridors hundreds of years ago, and if any of them remained.

This was my first experience working as a waitress. I learned how to make Melba toast, which supposedly had been created for Elizabeth Taylor so she had small snacks to nibble on. I became a master at mixing Irish coffees and learned how to cut and create melons for entrees, along with tasting a few of the English delicacies and weird tit-bits like roll-mop herrings.

On our afternoons off work, we wandered down to the famous castle Hampton Court on the banks of the River Thames. When we had two or more days off at a time we had time to travel further to socialize and explore London. On our train trips it was strange seeing houses like Coronation Street, which we had only seen on television back home.

Once overseas, the companionship of other New Zealanders seemed more important. We made friends and visited the local haunts where our country folk hung out. On Anzac Day, the normal tradition from home was celebrated in Wembley Rugby Hall, and we went along. Little did I know the after affect of the evening would change my life.

I spotted a guy that I wanted to dance with, but this never happened. Instead, his friend William came and asked me for a dance, and so I sealed my fate. I couldn't say no and was happy to have been rescued from being a wallflower. Apparently it is hard for other people to imagine this about me now, but at the time I had become one of those people who hung back. It was the stance I had taken since high school bullying.

Over the coming months we became an item. The boys purchased a double seated Ford Transit Van and were building bunks in the back for traveling to Europe. They invited us to travel with them. One of the girls decided to travel with her boyfriend which left three of us girls joining the boys. We planned our itinerary and finally were on our way to Europe.

Three weeks into our three-and-a-half month trip and life became edgy. The old habits of socializing in London with locals from home at the local taverns in the camps continued. It was fun, except three people partied every night until three in the morning. However, it interfered with our traveling and we were never ready to hit the road until nearly noon the next day. Things worsened at Pamplona with the running of the bulls and instead of two days, the majority out-voted the minority and we stayed a week. Discontent grew and tempers flared. I had worked and saved to come to Europe to visit new countries and learn about their history, culture and people. Consequently, when my traveling companions spent time drinking in tavernas with other New Zealanders I said that they may as well be back in New Zealand. I wanted to travel and so did William, so eventually, our group split.

With three people deciding to individually team up with others, William and I were left with the van to travel around Europe. It guzzled our budget for gas, split two ways instead of the five as previously planned. However, we completed the trip with a shortened itinerary, covering our basic costs with nothing left for souvenirs or luxuries. I visited as many art galleries with the famous paintings I had learned about from art history as I could.

We spent an eventful winter working in London before our journey back to Australia where we traveled via Asia on a conducted tour. It was another ford transit van and on this trip we slept in cheap hotels rather than the van. Our group consisted of ten people from a variety of countries with the oldest person being a seventy year old lady. It was exciting and completely different from Europe. Traveling via Iran and Iraq and experiencing a totally different culture, lifestyle and way of life was mind boggling.

We had a three day journey through the desert of death where we couldn't get any water. I was forced to drink Coca Cola, which I hate! Every mouthful was a challenge. During the trip we double dosed our water with purifying tablets to ensure it was germ free to drink. We didn't share our bottles of water like others did—who frequently had bouts of diarrhea and other stomach bugs which they spread amongst themselves.

It was interesting coming through the Khyber Pass. We were told not to take photos as any glimpse of reflection from the camera, could get us in trouble. It was our driver that caused our group to split on this trip. He was smuggling Japanese silk in the tent bags on the roof of the van. As we crossed the border from Pakistan into Indian the custom officers confiscated the van and arrested our driver. We never saw him or the van again and had to organize our own travel arrangements across India to Katmandu where we received a meager refund. We explored the city and although were scheduled to fly around Mt. Everest, it never occurred as clouds hung around the mountain for a week. Eventually we had to move on and connect with our pre-booked flights.

Our next destination was Perth in Australia, where William's family lived. Perth did not impress me with the dead brown grass, flies every-where and soaring temperatures. I adopted the Aussie wave, swishing flies from my face and checking my food before I took a bite at barbeques.

Life suddenly became normal as we didn't have to save for our next trip. We didn't have the social life like London or interesting places to visit. Our life together slipped into a more permanent relationship. Getting a job back in my original career path of fashion was a challenge. Life became boring and mundane which bred inner discontent and the thought that I was missing out on an adventure.

Eventually I decided to follow my passion of traveling. I started studying a travel course and passed all my subjects with great results. I become a travel agent, which I loved. I also decided to start a public speaking course. In hindsight, I have no idea why my first presentation was about the Taj Mahal. I was a nervous wreck. My face went bright red, my hands were sweaty and my voice shook. However I eventually conquered my fear as this is now my career and business.

As a New Zealander, I longed for a beach with some character of rocks and pools with interesting things around the corner in the next bay. Unfortunately for me, there were no beaches like that close to Perth. The main beach was beautiful white sand stretching for miles, which many people loved. The surf was beautiful, but I was not confident in the big waves. In the afternoon, the Fremantle Doctor rolled in. It was a weird name for the afternoon wind which blew the sand into whirly winds which stung my face and legs. By the time I arrived home after my trip to the beach I was hot again and it felt like I had never been near the water.

From August to October, Perth blossomed into a colorful paradise with the wildflower season. Unbelievably awesome flowers pushed themselves out of the dirt dry brown ground. Overlooking the city was Kings Park which grew thousands of Kangaroo Paw flowers. They had three to four green spikes and a red one and stood about a metre high. They were majestic looking and Western Australia's national flower. My favorite was a flower which only grew to about six inches high with green and purple petals; the colors of an avocado. The flower had four or five petals about an inch long each and on the edge crinkled up and resembled lace. These were the best months to live in Perth.

I didn't realize exactly what was happening. I was having health problems and still not happy. I found myself wanting to be rescued from my life. I found a book called *I'm Ok, You're Ok* by Thomas A. Harris, which explained a process called Transactional Analysis. I read it from cover to cover and it clarified why I was feeling so 'blue.' The author explained our relationship. It was a lose/lose relationship. I had become a peacemaker; keeping others happy but not making myself happy. The book provided solutions to move forward in life – and I was ready and willing.

I worked on change and making improvements. I thought our relationship was improving but in retrospection I was being manipulated. In hindsight it was a cop out. I didn't realize what I needed to do to create my own happiness, and it takes two people to make a relationship work. And, I was too nice for my own good and looked after other people first instead of myself.

Hindsight Insight

Learn to understand your feelings. Intuition and gut feelings are our inner compass and guide us. If we are not feeling okay it is a signal to ourselves we need to make change and say 'no' to something or someone in our life. As our feelings change to feeling okay it is an indication that we are getting on track in our life.

What are your feelings doing? Are you feeling okay or not? What do you need to learn or change in your life?

_____

_____

_____

_____

_____

_____

The process called Transactional Analysis in the book I'm OK, You're OK discusses different roles and types of relationships we experience, I didn't realise I was in a lose/lose relationship and getting bullied. Learning about this was a critical turning point in my life. It also provided me with a goal to achieve in my future relationships. I had to change. I still use this book with clients and the process in my workshops and coaching. The four relationships roles are lose/lose, win/lose, lose/win, win/win.

What are your present relationships scenarios? Do you need to make any changes?

_____

_____

_____

_____

_____

_____

Chapter 4

Disharmony and Bliss

Two robbers – Regret of the past - fear of the future.
—Fulton Oursler

We were starting to compromise and in 1981 we returned to New Zealand to get married in Huntly. On our wedding day, I had pre-wedding jitters. Someone told me this was normal and so I said 'yes' and my married life began. We had our honeymoon touring around New Zealand before traveling back to Perth.

I only wanted to have children close to my family and after a few years we returned to live in New Zealand. This was a compromise but there were still hiccups on the journey, and I kept hearing these 'bumps' were normal.

My most joyous moment was giving birth to our daughter Kirsty. I was working as a travel manager of a small wholesale travel company and worked until two weeks prior to giving birth. I was healthy and feeling fine.

Prior to giving birth I had decided that after six weeks I would return to work. However, I was not prepared for the life changing experience. I experienced such an overwhelming feeling of love for her that I was shaken into a new world. I fell in love with my daughter, which I suppose is the joy of becoming a parent for some people. I decided that noone could look after her as well as me. Although I had never changed a nappy and she was my guinea pig, at least the first nappy stayed up when we left hospital. Anyway, I gave up the notion of returning to work and instead decided to stay at home and be a full-time mother.

This was a real learning curve for me. In the past when anyone had spoken about children, I walked away. Up until then I had only been interested in travel and nothing else was important. Additionally, we had no young cousins or family members, so being a parent was really foreign to me.

Over our years of William and I living together, although I had tried to create a mutually rewarding relationship I continued to be a peacemaker. As I shared my ideas and thoughts I was being subtlety convinced into thinking I was wrong and my opinions were turned around to express the opposite. I was being manipulated and was unable to convince my point of view. I recall thinking, "I'm sure I didn't say that," many times. He would never accept we had a difference of opinion. He thought he was always right. Gradually I lost all confidence in myself and the decisions I made.

At dinner parties, I ceased entering into controversial discussions. After the visitors had left whenever I had a different opinion from William, the evening would end with a heated discussion. He thought a good partner and wife should agree with his ideas and solutions. Of course I didn't and eventually stopped having dinner parties so I could avoid playing the peacemaker. Instead I enjoyed time with my friends alone during the day.

William was a builder and one day an elderly lady who he was working with rang and commented and raved about how wonderful he was and how lucky I was to have him as a husband. After I got off the telephone, I questioned myself, whether I was wrong and she was right. I decided that I was the one who lived with him daily and although he could be nice at times, over time his manipulative and bullying behavior had made me lose more confidence in myself and become more submissive.

While I had been working, William had worked full time on our new house. After Kirsty was born we moved from our apartment around the corner and into the house. It was not properly finished, so I had many do-it-yourself jobs to complete when I had spare time during the day.

Along with learning how to be a mother, I had to learn how to stay at home. Always having been with adult company for all my working life, this became a challenge. During the day I would not speak to anyone outside the family. If I saw the neighbor, we could chat, but eventually I realised I needed more people contact to keep me sane.

One day I walked past Playcentre, which was in a new building up the road. I didn't know what Playcentre was, as my mother had always been in Kindergarten which our family had attended. However, when Kirsty was ten months old I joined became a Playcentre parent. This was to become another critical turning point in my life

I felt like sanity was returning. There were other parents I could talk to, toys for Kirsty to play with and other children to interact with. I felt like I had come home or found another place that felt like home. The ladies cared and chatted and I made new friends to replace the old ones from my working life. The philosophy behind it was to teach children through play, and then teach parents about helping their children to learn.

I did not realize it then, but Playcentre was a gift to me. I recall one day a lady (now my best friend, who I call an angel in disguise) suggesting I start the Playcentre training. She explained it would teach me about the stages of Kirsty's development, skills that were necessary for her to learn and help me with parenting. It was not long before I said yes, and a new learning curve began. I learned about different areas of play, why they were important, guidelines and boundaries, words and phrases to use and lots more that would help her development.

I enjoyed it so much, I moved onto the next phase. One of the exercises was to monitor how many times I said 'no' to her. I counted them for one hour. I had said 'no' fifty four times. I was shocked at myself. I thought I was protecting her whereas in reality I was stopping her learning boundaries and new experiences. Next I had to analyze how I could replace and rephrase some of those with more positive experiences for her. That was fabulous for me to learn. As a parent I needed to learn to *guide* her learning rather than *inhibit* her it.

It was not long before I was invited to be on the organizing team at Playcentre and use my new skills on the committee. Eventually I was invited to be a leader of the parenting courses. Next, I was 'shoulder tapped' again and invited to attend leadership courses. Eventually, I co-led the leadership groups. I loved this new found knowledge and started on my journey of personal development. In this great supportive environment, I thrived with the education.

I was blossoming, first with being pregnant again, but also with a new understanding about myself, parenting and people. Life was becoming clearer to me. During these few years I tried to adapt to married life but in hindsight a part of me was still unhappy.

The voices in my head were working in a strange way. I was having lots of negative thoughts about my marriage, self-esteem and self-worth.

The old saying, "not feeling good enough," bothered me. Why on earth I felt like that, I didn't know back then. One time I recall thinking that I was lucky anyone wanted to marry me at all. I thought this was as good as life could get, but marriage and children were not making me happy.

I could not defend myself verbally at home. I became more submissive in some areas and not in others. I withdrew from conversation rather than pre-empting any new ideas. Rather than cause an argument, I would say I that didn't know or didn't care, figuring that it was better than having a fight. I stood up for my daughters as much as I could, while they huddled together as we had an argument. Seeing them like that was one of the images that prompted me to make a move. I realized our relationship would never get any better, no matter how I tried, I needed a different solutions.

I was quickly learning about personal development and still had a huge amount to learn. I was a passive communicator and William was an aggressive one. I wanted to become an assertive communicator and wanted to continue to create a win/win relationship instead of a win/ lose one. We had counseling and William was convinced it was one hundred percent my fault. I was willing to accept half of the blame, but he was adamant that he was completely in the right. Eventually he stopped attending.

I was learning who I was, but enjoying more of who I wanted to become. Along with all the negative thoughts I also had over-riding thoughts telling me I was okay. Often, I felt I had three voices in my head, with the last one telling me I was good enough and I was worthy of having a better and therefore happier life than I was experiencing in life. Thankfully, eventually I believed it.

Someone made a comment to me that he doesn't drink, gamble,

womanize, smoke and a few other things, but that I could just not live with him. I had tried . . . and was failing. There was one way to do things in our house and it was his! Years later, I learned that people who don't like themselves have low self-esteem as well. The only way they feel good about themselves is when they are constantly putting someone else down. This builds their ego and makes them feel good (albeit from a negative action), but eventually it can destroy the other person.

With the knowledge I have now, I realize that bullying continued happening. Not the physical or spiritual but mental and emotional bullying. However, again I realize now that it takes two people and I didn't have the knowledge, skills and confidence to stand my ground and in fact should have left the relationship earlier. Still, it was lessons I needed to learn from back in my school days.

I hadn't planned this solution and I made plum jam the night before I left. One day, the time just felt right!

Hindsight Insight

It is a privilege to become a parent to a newborn infant who totally depends on us for their life. When you become parents you need to learn how to be a good parent. In many ways it is harder today because of the input from television and computers. Thus it is more critical to learn positive parenting skills. Society today has changed tremendously from when you were a child. First you need to learn to become your best and then teach your children. We assume we are 'doing the right thing.' We need to learn when to encourage, when to discourage and how we pass that onto our children so they become positive contributing members in society.

If you are a parent are you parenting well? If not, where can you learn more?

_____

_____

_____

_____

_____

_____

From our biggest challenges come our greatest lessons. One theory is that we create experiences in our life so we can learn to overcome them. I believe we are being supported in both our physical and spiritual world which is guiding us towards aligning our soul (feelings), mind (thoughts) and body (actions).

Are your mind, body and soul aligned to create the best you? What changes do you need to make?

_____

_____

_____

_____

_____

_____

Chapter 5

Plum Jam

Life will be to a large extend what we ourselves make of it
—Samuel Smiles

Plum Jam . . . I don't know why I cooked it . . . yet I do know. I had bags of ripe plums I could leave to rot or I could make jam for our future. It was the state of my mind at the time, *'betwitch and between,'* another phrase for confusion, fear, relief, courage and excitement.

Mum had always cooked plum jam the night before we went on our Christmas holiday because the plums became ripe. With a family of four children to feed, not having jam throughout the year was a big blow to our taste buds. So my association with plum jam was about family embarking on a journey with the household in a confused state of packing. The next morning we would be up early packing last minute essentials into the family car.

Subsequently in my case, the plums had to be cooked before I left on my adventures. Another family phrase I'd grown up with was *'waste not, want not.'* It was from Mum's childhood years in the 1930's and 1940's depression when food was scarce and when they didn't have the luxuries we have today. Consequently if I didn't use the fruit it meant my plums would have been wasted. In later years, I learned to freeze them.

Making the plum jam meant I was physically in a state of business and my mind was free to plan. And that's exactly what it was doing. Thinking through the 'for' and 'against' before I made my big move!

Racing through my mind were questions like: *Was I able to carry out my plan? Would I still have the courage in the morning? Could I get away without being spotted? What would happen after he came home? How would I manage?*

Sleep did come easily that night but when dawn broke the day was sunny. I needed to be ready for an exciting, scary, fearful and yet fearless journey. Was I ready? I was and I wasn't.

Just like when we went on the family vacation . . . the plum jam sat on the bench the next morning; freshly made and the kitchen smelt lovely and sweet and dare I say it jammy!! Doing the final stages of labeling and putting the lids on the jars was another preoccupation ensuring I kept out of harm's way and busy physically so mentally I could run through my plans again.

My children were their normal selves. Just what you'd expect a three year old and eighteen-month-old toddler to do in their morning routines. They wanted food and attention. Little did they know, mum's mind was in overload and they had one of the biggest shocks coming up in their young lives! Still, I had thought it through and decided it was better to have them growing up with one positive parent in a one parent family rather than two parents that constantly fought and where both parents were unhappy. Albeit, one happy parent and one unhappy negative parent would at least give them a choice about how they could live the rest of their lives when they became independent.

Their father left for work for the day and I went into overdrive. The bags were pulled from under the bed, the cot, highchair, stroller, toys, clothes, and the children's car seats were stashed into my small Toyota. My sanity had disappeared by now. There was definitely no room for any extra people to come along for a joy ride.

Breaking the news to my mother at eight o'clock was a drama. Talking through her tears, I'm not sure if it was a relief or shock at what I was doing. One of my friends had known I was going to leave. To the rest of the world, I appeared happily married but to some of my family members, a different girl from whom they had known in the past.

Our daughters and I were always welcomed with open arms at our family and relatives events. But my husband, that was another matter. He did not smoke, gamble, womanize, dished out no domestic violence, paid the bills, provided for his family, was not overweight or ugly, dressed nicely, appeared well mannered, but as someone said you just can't live with him. And that was true!

He was a bully and that is hard to detect. No physical abuse, but instead mental and emotional abuse. The type of abuse that cannot be seen by physical marks and only appears through unusual behavior.

Back to final crunch time. I had been finalizing my plan during the jam making process. I probably had other plans but my mother suggested I go somewhere I could not be found. So our cat and mouse journey began.

It was like a television program but this was my real-life drama unfolding. My sister had recently moved into a new home and it was decided we would go there. I needed to visit another sister's neighbor to collect a map to our destination.

I kept checking the driveway and listening to ensure no-one came home unexpectedly. There are a few times I blessed television and this was one of them. At least my daughters were occupied while I got organized.

Then came the moment of no return. Everything was in the car, then the last minute preparations with toddlers, the toilet stop, and drink, food and toys close at hand to keep them occupied. Finally I had the courage (and it took some) to walk out of my marriage and close the door behind me. I was taking a giant leap of faith in myself to begin a new life as a single parent. It wasn't on my 'to do list' of life . . . but here I was!

I drove around the back streets, I didn't want to see anyone I knew. The car was packed to the brim. In the 1960's there was a television programme called The Hillbillies. They had a truck packed high with household furniture as they moved into the city after making millions in an oil well on their country property. I felt a bit like that. Although I didn't have furniture quite hanging out of the car windows, I felt like I was in a jumble and unfortunately, I didn't have their millions either.

Getting gas felt like another major crisis. I went to a gas station I didn't normally visit so that I wouldn't see any familiar faces. It was our last stop and then we were onto the highway. Courage had gotten me there. Survival of the fittest—or the sanest—I'm not sure.

I would like to say that we had our windows down, the sun was shining on the hood of my newly polished car, the music was blaring, the wind billowed through our hair and we sang girl songs of the moment, *"the wheels of the car go round and round, round and round, round and round, the wheels of the car go round and round . . . "*

I am sure we didn't sing that song or the wind billowed through our hair . . . but the relief was immense. A huge weight was off my shoulders as I began the next most challenging phase of my life. I now had the opportunity to find me again and to create a brand new life for the girls and myself.

And so it was, after living in New Zealand for a few years, I finally had the courage to walk away from my marriage. A cousin later told me she was surprised because I had looked happy. My reply was—I was a good actress!

At thirty-three, I had the freedom to start a new era of my life. I was searching to rediscover the person I had lost when I was fifteen.

In those years, I eventually learned about self esteem, bullying, transactional analysis and creating win/win relationships. Prior to that lesson I had enjoyed life, but behind the façade of a smiling face. I was a lost soul, searching for happiness and waiting to be rescued, not knowing I had to rescue myself!

Hindsight Insight

Family traditions, beliefs and values affect us from our past. Some are helpful and support us whilst others are damaging to our future when 'words and actions' no longer are relevant to our present goals. It is important to examine and clear up experiences from the past. Often we need to understand and then forgive ourselves and others as we redesign our life. We need to retain 'what makes us feel good' and dismiss what is unaligned. I had to rethink my beliefs about leaving my marriage and becoming a single parent with my children not living full-time with their father. Eventually I decided my beliefs no longer supported my situation and had to rethink my values.

Do you have any past traditions, beliefs, values or experiences that need to be re-examined to allow you to move forward to a more positive way of thinking?

_____

_____

_____

_____

_____

_____

Bullying is soul destroying. It happens in homes, communities, schools, government and workplaces worldwide. It can be subtle and undetected physically or it can be brutal and visible with broken bones and bodies. It affects those with low self-esteem, and unassertive and people who have little personal awareness skills. Some people have this challenge from childhood or it could be one situation that affects their thinking. Unaware in my teenage years, I started living like that and continued in relationships expecting the same types of support and love I had in my childhood. My unhappiness grew and I wanted to be rescued to get my life back on track. I searched for solutions and eventually found it in changing my thoughts and becoming a single parent rather than be bullied.

If you rated your present level of self esteem from one to ten, what number would you rate yourself? I suggest if it is below five then start learning about how to raise your self-esteem. Join courses, read books and begin this journey. Above five, continue working towards your goals and dreams, ensuring they are values aligned to you. If you rated eight and above, congratulations! Your new role is to 'shoulder-tap' and help others on their journey.

Chapter 6

Not A Goal

*It takes a lot of courage, it calls for strength of mind, to make a
new beginning and leave the past behind. To build upon the ruins,
to dream another dream. To set forth in the darkness to-wards a
distant gleam. To suffer many losses, yet faithful to remain.
To rise about disaster and then begin again.*

—Unknown

It had taken me a lot of courage to make my decision to leave my
marriage and follow it through. I was creating a new life for us
and there was no going back. Apparently William came home
that night with a bunch of flowers for me, but instead found my
note.

At my sister's new house where she had moved in a week earlier, I
felt safe. Anne had found room for us at short notice and it was like
an adventure for the girls. She was on school break and over the
next few days had lots of visitors. Each night over drinks at cocktail
hour a different set of visitors arrived and I discovered most of the
people had been divorced. I realized I was doing something they
had done before and I didn't feel so uncomfortable. Additionally,
everyone was very encouraging about my new future.

During these discussions, the truth was finally revealed how my
family, friends and relations wondered how I could have stayed
with William for so long.

After a week away I returned to Auckland to stay with a girlfriend.
She lived a few streets away from our house and it gave the girls the

opportunity to visit their father.

William was convinced I was going to return. In my attempt to disrupt the girls the least, I thought he would move out of the house so they could continue to live in their home and attend their local Playcentre. That was naive thinking on my behalf. He was angry and assured me of future challenges.

One of my worst experiences was when I had to enroll for child support. I was the only European in the room and felt humiliated and more like a failure than ever. I started the divorce proceedings which also involved some counseling. At one of these sessions, I decided I would revert back to my maiden name. The counselor supported the idea but William abused him and stormed out of the session. I was advised that the best I could do while the girls were with me was to ensure I provided a warm happy positive home for the three of us.

That was not going to happen quickly in Auckland, and we moved to live with my parents up at Snells Beach. We lived in the rooms in the basement which was already set up with beds, bathroom and cooking facilities. It was another adventure, with the girls and I joining the local Playcentre. I had regular trips to down to visit the lawyers. It was organized that the girls would live with me and on every second weekend would go and visit their father. We met at the playground area in Orewa and the girls would leave for a weekend away and I would return to Mum and Dad's.

After six months I organized to move back into the house, got a second mortgage and bought the house from him. I thought it was better that the girls stayed in the area with their friends and in their home.

Once back in the house Dad built a concrete path for us and when the girls were away I spent weekends painting and worked on finishing the house. After a few months I was worn out and learned to pace myself. I discovered being a single mum with two toddlers and the challenges with William was exhausting. I finally realized that during the weekends they were away I had to chill out and have some rest. I didn't have to get up at six every morning, and instead could lie in bed and read a book.

In the early days of our divorce, I was still allowing William to come into the house. I was ironing and because I didn't agree with him, he threatened me and pinned me up against the ironing board. I managed to free myself and went out onto the street until he came out of the house. After that incident, I refused to allow him into the house. He always threatened me that he "would get me" whenever he wanted. He had built the house and no doubt could break in very easily. I finally came to the conclusion I couldn't live my life packaging myself in cotton wool, or I would become a prisoner to his threats.

As time progressed, a number of incidents occurred. Once I had to get investigated and although I will never know the real answer, it was something that as a mother I had to check out. It meant access was stopped for a few months, but as I followed the advice of the 'experts' I decided they were experienced with these situations and I wasn't.

I was always searching for some direction. A girlfriend suggested I visit a clairvoyant. I had never been to one and was very skeptical. I wasn't quite sure how they worked or where they got their information from. I assumed it was the 'spirit' world in some way, but I wasn't quite sure how. When it was my turn the clairvoyant asked what sort of direction I was looking for. I explained I was having a few challenges and worried about the girls. She asked for my birthday and also the girl's birthdates.

"What does he think he is doing?" she said suddenly. "He is playing silly games!"

I hadn't told her about the challenges I was having with their father. "It's time he grew up and put his daughters first," she commented. Then she told me that my daughters had so much of 'me' in them and very little of their father, so they would be fine.

I was impressed with her insights into my life, when I had been very careful not to reveal any specific information. I had wanted to 'test' her so I could analyze whether she was really performing a reading or guessing her answers. I left her house with a new respect about clairvoyants.

In hindsight, whatever messages and insights they access for their clients, as long as they focus on the positive I can't see any harm in getting peace of mind and clarity for one's future. Life moves in ebbs and tides and generally people only visit for a reading if they are in ebb, and they are always looking for answers to when their tide will turn. On our journey everyone has challenges in all different areas of life, so any mention of a challenge that has to be overcome is not a new message, just reassuring the person to be resilient and keep learning and growing. Any idea that concentrates someone's thinking on the positive, is leading them towards their success and happiness more proactively.

Many of William's and my new disputes were about parenting. I had joined Playcentre and started learning about parenting because I didn't know how to be a good parent. William had expected Kirsty to recite the alphabet at two years old like a parrot and was adamant she ate all her dinner, hungry or not.

My philosophy was quite different and I had learned about the importance of being a positive influence in the girl's lives. William scoffed at this and was full of anger towards me and anything I suggested. He was forthright in condemning me; swearing and told me he was praying to God that I was dead. He called me the devil and other negative words and behavior in front of the girls. Although I asked him to stop this, he refused.

I decided I had to find another approach because the verbal abuse affected me and although the girls said they didn't listen, I was sure his action and words would affect them. Eventually I stopped these abusive sessions by having the girls' bags at the front door when he arrived. I hugged them before they went out the door and waved goodbye from the front window as they drove away in the car. They hardly ever looked, only occasionally taking a glance and never waved back, but at least I thought they had seen me.

It was not a nice feeling, but it stopped the insults towards me in front of the girls. I had no control of what he said to them, although I had control of what I did. I didn't believe what he said but it wasn't fair that he hurt the girls with his words. He didn't seem to care.

When the girls arrived back home on Sunday nights at six, they always distanced themselves from me. Their hugs and kisses were directed at the cat who was neutral territory for them. Eventually, when they settled in bed, they were ready to give me a hug. I could understand how they felt, not knowing who to believe and what to feel, so I let them work at their own pace. It was usually nine o'clock before they fell asleep.

Another incident occurred when I was working in the garage where I had moved my small business. The girls had told me that relatives from Australia were coming to visit. The week before they arrived, William asked to take the girls from school so they could go for a vacation. I refused but said they could stay with him but had to attend school. That wasn't the answer he wanted. He thumped in the side of my car and he threatened to kill me. I ran inside and called the police. They arrived and took him away.

Later the episode was in court and I applied for a restraining order so that he couldn't come onto the property. He had always threatened to hurt me and when the court refused I was devastated and scared. It took a month of crying to come back to the realization, that if he was going to really hurt me, he probably would have already done it. I also realized if he carried out his threats he probably would not see the girls again, which I am sure he didn't want.

In fact, I had to get over his threats, my fear and get on with life. I decided my time in life was up when it was up! I had lots of living to do, so I had to get on with it.

It was about this time that I read the book, *Feel the Fear and Do it Anyway,* by Susan Jeffers.

Immediately after this court decision, William applied for full custody. Until now the girls lived with me, but visited their father every Wednesday night for dinner and every second weekend from five o'clock on Friday to five o'clock Sunday evenings. He always got angry if we were a minute late, even if it was the girls messing around or we were held up in the traffic, however he would not listen and continued with his abuse.

When our case finally went back to court, I had a lawyer and William decided he would speak for himself. At that stage my lawyer said it was probable the girls would be granted to spend one week with their father and one week with me. I thought that would be harder for them, so I offered for them to stay on the Sunday and Wednesday nights instead of coming home. That allowed him to take them to school on the following mornings. It was granted but again, I cried for a month, as I was now giving the girls a life where the longest they stayed in their home was six nights before they were packing bags and on the move again. Eventually I realized I was more worried about it than them, and relished the time out for me.

During these times I earned extra money from babysitting until I had enough money to purchase second-hand carpet for the house. I had all the under felt and spent a complete weekend laying it down on the floor so I would save some of the carpet layer's fee. As soon as he opened the door, he informed me I had laid it all upside down. I was deflated!

William had built the house and although I had purchased it from him, he continued to refer to it as his house. This started to grate on my nerves, as the girls would always say the fruit trees and everything were so good because their dad had planted them. I realized it was not their fault, he probably was reminding them, but finally I decided I had to move away from the negative energy. I went searching for another answer.

Hindsight Insight

Your support system is creating win/win relationships with your family and friends. These are the people who help you and who you also help. Some people are known as 'takers' who just use people and others are the 'helpers.' In creating your system, it is generally an unconscious move but find mutually rewarding relationships rather than one-sided ones.

Who is your support system? If you don't have one, what action do you need to undertake to establish one?

When events happen that you don't like, there is always action you can take. You are only in control of yourself, no-one else, therefore if something doesn't feel right; ask yourself the question – 'why does this not suit me, my values or life rules'. You are likely to uncover your reason and then take positive action to create a different outcome.

Have you got any situations that make you feel uncomfortable? What do you need to rethink so you can change your actions?

Chapter 7

Staying Sane

*Anybody can become angry - that is easy, but to be angry with the
right person and to the right degree and at the right time and for
the right purpose, and in the right way - that is not within every-
body's power and is not easy.*

—Aristotle

The counselor told me to create a warm and loving home for
the girls and that is what I did. Many visitors commented on
the lovely feeling within the house. I could not explain it as
I didn't have new or grand furniture. At the start I had no carpet,
only linoleum, on the wet areas in the house. Maybe it was the
sense of peace that now pervaded the house. Anyway, it felt good
and it was mine, second mortgage and all.

In the early days of moving back to our house, I had a rude awakening. Along with learning to handle what mum called 'hell hour'
which was dinner time from five to six when we were all tired, I was
having the custody challenges.

One day, when I was upset, tired and angry from the lawyers and
William's demands, I recall almost tipping over the edge. Kirsty did
something wrong and in a split second I almost smacked her for
a reason that was way beyond what was needed. I usually never
smacked them, instead reprimanded them with words or actions, so
I was surprised at myself. In that instant I decided I needed a new
strategy. I found seventy-nine dollars from our budget and the next
day went and purchased a second hand video machine.

From that day onwards, I had a collection of movies or television program taped, so when we were all tired the girls could watch them while I prepared dinner. Normally television was only watched from five in the evenings onwards unless it was a real treat, or I was either sick or exhausted. On Saturday and Sunday morning, they were allowed to watch the early programmes before breakfast. After that television was turned off for the day and never on in the mornings once the girls were of school age.

An earlier strategy when the girls were old enough to be left alone was playtime in the bath was with toys, colored water, bubbles, ice cubes and other activities that kept them amused while I cooked tea.

In the early days of single parenting I decided two things to continue. First, a glass of wine for myself and second, keep gas in the car so I could visit people. After spending all day with children and no adult company coming home at night to chat to, my treat was to sometimes have a glass of wine at night while I prepared the dinner. This turned 'hell hour' into a time I could organize the girls and treat myself, I had survived another day and was still sane. (I think!)

I became friends with Trish who lived around the corner and on Friday nights would often visit her for a combined tea and with our five kids. Her husband owned a restaurant and worked at night and we would get together for our social time.

Another fun and relaxing time when I had the girls in the weekends was when we would go boating and stay overnight with Mum and Dad. Our family loved being on the sea and the enjoyment was passed onto the girls.

In a two parent's family running a household, the jobs are shared but with only one parent, I had to be very organized. After rushing around to finish the housework, packing the car, food and getting organised, I then flopped into the car for an hours drive. We would arrive a little after ten. Mum would send me to help Dad bring the boat to the wharf while the girls would help pack the lunch and carry things to the car for Nana.

Dad and I would motor up the channel in the dinghy to get Dreamer off her mooring. We would take her back to Sandspit wharf where Mum and the girls had usually arrived. They would climb aboard with the lunch and all the gear and we would disembark for a day's adventure. We would chug out the channel and before we hit the open seas Mum made hot coffee and homemade cooking for morning tea. I was always craving for this and to me it was a signal I could relax for the day. There was someone else to share responsibility for the girls for a few hours as we headed towards our favorite bay, Mansion House Bay on Kawau Island.

Mum and Dad loved fishing and there was always a competition between Poppa and the girls about who caught the first, most and biggest fish. The girls always seem to win as Dad didn't have much time for fishing himself after baiting and organizing everyone else's' fishing line. I was happy to relax and read the newspaper while everyone enjoyed fishing. Usually we went home every night but one time we did stay on the boat, I woke to find Leila missing from her sleeping bag. She had quietly gotten out of bed, hooked her line and was sitting on the bow of the boat, trying to catch more fish than Poppa had the day before.

Mansion House on Kawau Island was always our favorite lunchtime spot. The girls had learned to swim and once they were old enough, they climbed into the dingy. We gave them a few sandwiches and a drink and with their lifejackets on and a rope attached to Dreamer as they floated around the back of the boat eating their lunch. We pulled them in when lunch was over and eventually taught them to row the dinghy, so they could have small adventures while we could watch them. Usually after lunch we went ashore for a walk in the beautiful gardens, looking for wekas, wallabies and the peacocks.

Mansion House itself oozes grace and serenity. The magnificent two story house, built from last century, has a beautiful garden with plants collected from around the world. Once when we picnicked on shore we were entertained by the Tuis drunk on the nectar from the flowers from one of the magnificent trees. They almost fell out off the branches after they had their fill from the flowers and in the nick of time just before they hit the ground regained, their flying skills only to go soaring off, squawking madly, high up into the sky.

Afternoons on Dreamer were always fishing, swimming, or finding a new adventure in a different bay to visit. On the journey home, if I was driving back to Auckland that night, the back cabin was always my bed as I had a half hour snooze while the girls were entertained.

If we did stay overnight, a family tradition was Dad would get up and make the morning cup of tea, I would climb into their bed and we were delivered two lovely cups of tea and biscuits. The house had been designed so the master bedroom and lounge looked out over Kawau Bay, and it was lovely sitting in bed looking at the view. Over the years the numbers and size of grandkids grew but the tradition remained and we have many photos with the bed crowded with kids, gone in for a cup of tea and a chat with Nana. On sunny days, sunglasses have been worn, which again have made some great photos and memories.

On a trip to Europe Dad had found the music for the Bird Dance. By the second cup of tea if the grandchildren hadn't emerged from their beds in the basement, the music would be turned on and that was the signal, with Poppa dancing upstairs that it was time to 'get out of bed' and ready for a days boating. This song became one of his signature songs and was eventually played at his funeral, again with us all dancing as we celebrated his life.

After a few times when we had stayed away and the girls had wanted something different to wear, I made a decision they had to learn to pack their own clothes. Each weekend they were away and clothes returned home for washing, they were repacked in bags ready for their next excursion. Eventually I did this for myself as it was saving me double handling my clothes once I went away sailing.

There was never spare money and I lived on a strict budget. We never went hungry and only had take-away food as a birthday treat. My motto was to have frozen dinners ready if I was tired or we came home late. I decided an occasional meal of poached eggs or a tin of baked beans for dinner was fine and we would catch up on our vegetables another night.

Mum and Dad continued to visit, which was great. Sometimes in summer they would stay for dinner so they could see the girls after school. Our family tradition was playing the piano while Mum cooked tea, so when they stayed she would take over the kitchen again and Dad and I would have a sing song, accompanied by the girls. Our Welsh heritage meant music was important to Dad and I included it in the girls after school activities with organ and guitar lessons. At school they played the recorder and Leila tried out the saxophone, and they performed in many school talent performances.

I fell into starting my first business after I had used my dressmaking skills from a previous career, into making a dress-up costume for Leila. Understanding about the importance of learning through play for the development of the girls, I expanded this philosophy at home.

We had a playhouse, swing, seesaw, sandpit, climbing frame in the backyard and during the summer often the plastic swimming pool outside. I had also allowed the girls during a creative moment, dig a fish pond and they helped in the garden, painting and outside maintenance work. I had learned the power of learning through play and the girls were involved in as many things as I could find. I was often asked if I ran a childcare center at home.

With dramatic play being important, inside the house we also had a table and chairs with an array of toys, costumes, and learning activities. I remember thinking that I was attending too many meetings when the girls, during their drama play, were actually playing 'going to meetings.' I had some consolation when most of the meetings were at other Playcentres, and the girls came and played while it was in progress.

The first costume I made was to support Leila's passion for cats. I had some black and white striped jersey material from a sale and made her a cat suit. With a tail and matching hood with fluffy back, velvet years, Leila lived in this suit for almost two years until she grew out of it. Worn to Playcentre, out shopping, to bed, around home, she lived and breathed the life of a cat whilst in her suit. Drinks of Milo were lapped from a saucer on the floor and she replied to my questions with meows.

We had a cat which both the girls loved and whenever we were anywhere with animals, Leila was likely to be playing with them. From a young age, Leila had a special affiliation, passion and natural talent with animals, which eventually led to her career as a vet nurse.

Clarie's dress up costume was a purple fairy dress with wings. She loved her outfit and for her fourth birthday we had a fairy castle cake, which as a twenty year old, she still claims was her favorite. All the Playcentre children wore different dress up costumes to her party and gradually my dress up business Funtasia Fashions was born.

Mothers asked me to make costumes for their childrens favorite character and gradually I was expanding my costumes into a small business. I started supplying them to Edmonton Playcentre, and then other centers. Prior to this dress up clothes were adults clothes cut down for the children to wear.

As an ex-dressmaker, the hardest thing was to make the costumes simple. I was used to sewing wedding dresses for a real bride to wear, so making a costume that would allow it to become a profit-making affair was a learning curve. I incorporated colour coded Velcro so the children could learn their colours and get praised for putting the costume on themselves . . . thus boosting their self esteem.

My sewing machine cabinet was in the corner of the dining room where I first made the costumes. Gradually it took over the dining room table until I decided it was time to graduate into my garage. It didn't have any electricity connected out there . . . so the family went into 'solution' mode for me.

We often had the Christmas parties at my house because it was midway between Warkworth and Huntly. My brother-in-law who was an electrician decided to put electricity into the garage for me. They also decided to install my security lights. I didn't have any ladders and so they carried over our very heavy see-saw and with the wife sitting on one end, her husband was levered high enough to reach the lights. A photo I will treasure for ever!

Dad built me a large cutting table with shelves and storage and over seven years my first small business grew. Gradually, I established a shop in there and with both girls at school my days were spent running the business.

I employed a machinist with an industrial machine to make the costumers. I did the designing, cutting and sales. I sold them into Playcentres, childcare centres and kindergartens throughout New Zealand via direct marketing. I grew the business to thirty-five different costumes and had only one other company in Hamilton who was my only competition. I made a few trips to the South Island and tried to get a sales person down there.

Over the years, I grew the business from nothing to a turnover of $26,000. I attended local business courses to learn how to run a business. Some of the forecasts had the business growing globally.

During our Christmas parties, because I had a collection of clothes, this extended to all the nephews and nieces dressing up as well. However when it became time for Santa to wear his costume and it was time to share out the presents, they turned into Santa's elves. The costumes would get traded for all the red clothes, hats and belts that could be found in my wardrobe and drawers that helped change them into his helpers.

One year my sister decided to continue this theme and every child and Nana and Poppa received a navy blue sweatshirt with a hood which had Dreamer, their boats' name embroidered on it. For years these were worn out boating.

But something was changing. I decided the business was never going to be enough to support us. I started to miss adult contact and I was getting bored, discontent and unhappy. Eventually, I sold the business to a friend and had a change of career as I became a gardener for a few months while I contemplated my future.

Hindsight Insight

Anger is a good feeling because it is indicating that something is not okay in your life. First you need to analyze the situation and secondly you need to make some changes in your life. The challenge is to understand why you are angry and then vent your anger in the right direction.

Have you got any situations where you are angry which you need to analyse? Do you need to make any changes?

_____

_____

_____

_____

_____

_____

Managing stress is critical in our life. Being a busy person always leads me to burnout until I remember to juggle the stress and align myself to nature and learn to relax. The 'flight or fight' reflex is inherent within us from centuries ago. Our body reacts by increasing the tempo of our body's organs. It is important that you find some ways of release otherwise these pent up feelings will continue to circulate and aggravate your health.

Do you need to find new methods for stress management?

_____

_____

_____

_____

_____

_____

Chapter 8

Supported Becoming

A spinner of destiny, a weaver of dreams, a spider in her web represents these themes.
With care and patience all your dreams you weave, all goals are possible for you to achieve, in you, I believe.

—Unknown

Studying parenting through Playcentre, I meet lots of other parents and was invited into a babysitting club. We had a contra credit system based on time spend 'sitting' and this enabled me to babysit when the girls were away and have a babysitter if I needed one. The girls were my top priority, but joining the club allowed me my freedom to attend meetings or have a social life. Not that my social life was huge or much money was left in the budget, but it was a mindset, of not being trapped.

Even though I was a single mum I was accepted into the group. I became a threat to some ladies . . . who obviously thought I might be interested in their husbands. After getting rid of one, I had other things to sort out in my life that were more important.

Being a single parent meant another new set of skills were required. I seemed to be on a constantly learning curve and craving understanding and education which had started with my introduction at Playcentre. The babysitting club was helpful when we had any of my Playcentre committee meetings or parenting training meetings in the evening. Other ladies had their partners to babysit when we had an evening meeting, whereas for me the club was really useful.

I had continued my parenting education to the next level of Playcentre training. This moved up from areas of play to child psychology and human development. I was really interested and after learning about the seven year phases in life and still use this theory in my work today. This was helpful when I became a Playcentre supervisor as well as understanding the girls and myself.

As soon as I mastered one skill something else would catapult into my life. The library and friends were great sources of new books and information to borrow.

Gradually, I moved beyond Playcentre and started to look at more business groups. Someone introduced me to SWAP, which stood for Sales People with a Purpose. As my thirst and hunger for more information grew, I became involved and eventually joined onto the committee. I had learned to volunteer and was asked to write their monthly newsletter. Now, at this stage I had never been in a 'relationship' with a computer. When I had left Bridge Travel years ago in Perth, the computer was just starting to enter the world of travel. By volunteering it was putting myself on the line and forcing myself to learn how to use this contraption. I scraped together a few dollars and purchased a second hand one from one of the Playcentre parents.

For some reason I feared that I would never master this new skill. I had learned to type in high school, but now I was there turning it on and off, saving documents, fixing spelling, formatting and one million-two-hundred-fifty-trillion other things I had to learn and remember. It was overwhelming. I continued to remind myself the only way to learn and Nike's motto, "Just Do It," so I must.

With notebook and pen, I wrote down every step of the journey. I had pages of notes but it seemed that every time I had a problem, the answer was never anything I had encountered before and once again, was always searching for the solution. I decided only two things in my life had made me really angry. One was my ex-husband and I had rid myself of him but this computer I viewed differently. It was a door to my future and I needed to master it. Many times I felt like putting a hammer through it, but sense and calm was regained after a telephone call to a friend, and she would provide my solution. It was annoying to learn the computer was always right, and I was always wrong, there was only one way, and that was follow the steps and the systems. I was not a systems person, but I knew that I had to learn!

At the weekly SWAP meetings we had a speaker to motivate or share their story. One morning Brian Head, the hypnotist, was speaking and asked for a volunteer, someone who had a fear they wanted to conquer. Immediately my arm went up, and two seconds later I was sitting on the chair at the front of the room. I explained my fear of being unable to master the computer. He immediately 'did his thing,' and after I watched something move side to side in front of my eyes. I slipped into another world. When I awoke and focused my consciousness back to present and the group in front of me, I felt much more confident that I would master this new technology.

Consequently, for the first year in this role, the monthly newsletter was designed, written and distributed to the members. The following year, again someone saw skills in me, which I didn't myself. I was asked to become the Vice President and a year later voted in as President of the club. Through my personal development I had realized I was great at being a democratic leader and worked with creating a supportive team environment and achieving results. I followed on from an autocratic President and was offered support from the National President with any challenges that would arise. None did that I couldn't handle and after I had finished my term, another autocratic leader moved into the role. I was using all my Playcentre skills with business people and discovered the wealth of knowledge I had gained along with the ability to create a club that people wanted to join.

From the local club I was voted in as National Executive. Again this was a great learning curve in meetings, conferences, decision-making, more computer skills, telephone conferences and a myriad of other experiences in a supportive business environment.

I was learning every time I took a leap forward in life, and I excelled. As I developed and my confidence in myself grew and boosted my esteem up one notch further, I sought new boundaries for myself.

After selling my business and spending time soul-searching, I was also sailing almost every other weekend. It was a wonderful break after dropping the girls at their dad's to pick up my gear and have some time out for me. Often I would climb on board the yacht and a roast dinner would be cooked in the galley kitchen and I had an opportunity to chill out.

One long weekend, we sailed to Great Barrier. Another boat sailed over with us and we spent time together rafted up, chatting, socializing and enjoying the serenity of the island. My goal was to go ashore everyday to exercise and a lady from the other boat joined me.

We decided to climb Mt. Hobson, the highest mountain on the island. During our all-day hike we chatted and I learned the lady was looking for a person to teach travel to the students at her work. I shared my qualifications and experience and a few days after my arrival back home on dry land, I received a telephone call.

I was invited in for an interview and immediately got a job as a travel tutor. I hadn't known what I was searching for, but here was an opportunity to take a new direction in life and become fully independent. Consequently, it was a great day when I realized I was finally able to fully support my children and myself. With a minuscule amount of assistance from the other parent, it had been a constant financial challenge to survive and then attempt to thrive.

The girls were old enough for new routines and were walking to school, and I was confident they could look after themselves for short periods before I arrived home from work. I had chosen the part-time option as I always had them for half the holidays and any change to that would have caused a major problem. It would also have provided a great opportunity for an attempt at changes to the girls' custody. I did not want to take any chances with that.

Like any new job you always give your best. I was tutoring students for the work in the travel and tourism industries. I was employed on a reasonable good hourly rate for tutoring classroom hours and then planning and marking was to be in my own time.

The systems for passing exams was ridiculous and additional hours were wasted.

I was continuously supporting students who were not working properly in the classroom or doing homework, and then I had to tutor them individually so they would pass their courses. Some weeks I was working sixty hours and only getting paid for half that time.

I was supposed to write teaching plans, but I did them all in my head while I sat in the traffic morning and night to and from work. The biggest criticism I had from the students was I spoke too fast.

Initially I was hurt and disappointed as I had attempted to do a good job. However, I recalled a lesson from Playcentre leadership training, about 'The Gift.' As we develop our skills we receive feedback and have two choices. One theory is that you completely ignore it or secondly we place it on a shelf in our mind. Then, if we receive the same feedback a few more times, we need to examine the feedback as a gift and decide what changes we can make to ourselves. This is what I did eventually, and slowed down my speech.

Gradually, I learned to work smarter. The job suited me because I could drive the girls to school and pick them up afterwards, which saved forty dollars a week in bus fares. Also, I could have holidays off to look after them rather than them be at home alone. Eventually the rules were changed regarding resits for exams and as the workload pressure eased off. It was quite a few years before I received a two-dollar pay raise and they were still expecting additional time spent on meetings, correcting papers and an array of other tasks. I had become a negative worker because by now it was a real win/lose working relationship.

I stayed because it suited and became very quick at marking, getting organized and other work, thus allowing me time to spend while sitting in exam rooms doing my own work and writing, rather than wasting my time. I had managed to find a solution. They were paying me to sit in exam rooms for hours, so I took my laptop and did my work. In some ways I saw this as compensation for the hours of work I was doing with no pay.

Over the seven years I tutored full-time my classes always had a great team spirit. Again my Playcentre training came to use as I developed ground rules with each new group. My best rule was that everyday every student had to sit in a different place next to a different person. This eliminated any chance of cliques in the groups between races, ages and friends. One year I had nine different cultures in the classroom and they were aged from seventeen to forty-five years old. With my ground rule, they worked together well, supporting each other throughout their time together.

During these years, each group of students had an educational trip where they experienced some part of New Zealand. We had a teacher student ratio and traveled to the Bay of Islands, Rotorua, Wellington, Christchurch and Queenstown. One year the girls came with me to the Bay of Islands and another year I had a last minute cancellation and Mum came. The trips were hard work getting organized and supervising the students who sometimes got into mischief but they provided me with some adventures I otherwise wouldn't have been able to afford.

I taught my students more than their course work. My theory was that they needed to be confident if they worked in the travel industry. Consequently, my moving them around the classroom, along with daily opportunities for them to write on the board at the front of the room and activities where they were standing up front added to their confidence levels. It was great when one of the students was writing a word that he or she couldn't spell and someone would call out to help them.

I met some neat people and some weird people and it was wonderful to make a difference. Some students were in the right career path while others were wasting their time. I continued doing really parttime work for a few years which helped my transition from one stage of life into the next.

Unknown to me, at that stage I had been realigned to my 'true self' from when I was as a leader and teacher at primary school. People had shoulder-tapped me, or in fact the universe had reunited me. I had a got lost on my journey, found and followed my passions and now a lot more wisdom and knowledge . . . was tracking okay.

Hindsight Insight

Learning involves changing your thinking to embrace new ideas. We become more enthusiastic about life but it can be invigorating and frustrating. Learning the computer or any other new task is always easy for people who know how to use it. Looking out for ordinary answers is another way of to solve a problem. I had no idea I would get hypnotized but I jumped at the possibility of discovering a solution that could work. Visualizing, affirmations and any tools that help you change your thinking are useful.

If you are stuck in a problem, what right brained creative solution could you find that would help you?

_____

_____

_____

_____

_____

_____

Shoulder-tapping is the name I use when the universe, in either its physical or spiritual mode, steers us in a new direction. Our life goal is to become our best and usually we don't see our natural gifts and talents because they are easy for us. We get a paradigm shift in our thinking when it is suggested to us, we try some new experience in life. Ultimately they are leading towards our greatness and destiny. Going with the flow in life is when we say 'yes.'

When have you been shoulder-tapped in life and a) you have listened b) you didn't listen and need to revisit those suggestions?

_____

_____

_____

_____

_____

Chapter 9

Gratitude Lessons

Chasing rainbows does have pots of gold in the end.

—Anon

L ife was busy and every night the dishwasher went on. One eventful morning I woke to find the floor soaked throughout the kitchen and dining room. As I paddled my way in to view the damage, I realized the dishwasher had not worked properly and instead of the water going down the drain, it had leaked all over the floor. I quickly gathered towels to stop the water going onto the carpet in the hallway and lounge room as I didn't want to lose it because it had taken a lot of hard work for me to find the money to be able to afford second hand carpet for the house.

I called the girls to help me mop up the water. Leila wanted to wear her rain boots but I assured her it was not quite that deep. I called the insurance company and thankfully when the assessor arrived he said it would be covered under my insurance. Apparently the hot water cylinder thermostat broke and the boiling hot water had melted the connection to the dishwasher hose and consequently the water did not flow down the drain.

The insurance company sent a tradesman who brought along huge heaters to dry the carpet. It seemed my second hand carpet would stain and the new curtains had soaked up the water, meaning they might also be ruined. That night, a positive friend from SWAP called and I shared my worries with him. This was one of those critical turning points and real moments in my life. I remember the words, which I had heard before, *"There's always a silver lining in every cloud."* As everything appeared to be going wrong after the flooding, I couldn't see any silver lining myself.

In spite of this I was mistaken. The following day, the insurance assessor called and said he was currently working on another insurance claim. A large house with cream shag carpet had to be replaced and he wondered if I would be interested in re-carpeting my whole house with this carpet. Here was my silver lining – my second hand, nonmatching carpet was now going to be replaced with cream shag carpet, albeit still being second hand. Life was handing me something good . . . it felt great. When it was laid, the carpet made a huge difference, modernizing our home.

My Playcentre philosophy of children learning through play meant that as I cooked the meals I had started teaching the girls to cook as well. Consequently, I ate plenty of cans of baked beans, 'interesting' sandwiches, burnt toast and hamburgers until gradually I was getting a full meal cooked for me. From supervising the girls and standing next to them and watching them, to slowly allowing them cook a few things alone while I was in the house, was a progressive lesson in learning to cook.

Alongside the stove was an eighteen inch square of tiles for placing the hot pots on. The girls had been taught this. Unfortunately, one time Kirsty forgot that lesson and put a hot pot on the Formica. It was a corrugated style raised Formica and so the hot pot burnt the top and left a hole on my bench.

A few weeks later Mum was visiting and mentioned she thought it was covered by my insurance. Another telephone call and another positive outcome. So my second situation occurred when a few months later a different insurance assessor arrived and told me that the Formica would be replaced. Lucky for me, but probably not for him, I had a huge bench and also had the same Formica behind the stove, on my windowsills and in the cabinet with a glass front which held my dinner set. This Formica was about seven years old and so now I had an opportunity to have my complete kitchen redone with a newer style Formica.

For the second time that year, life was handing me something good . . . again it felt great!! Interesting lessons were starting to happen and I didn't realize it.

This year I was also busy involved being the President of North Shore SWAP group. I'd moved from being the President of a parenting group and an executive member of the New Zealand Playcentre Federation to now being president to the leader of a business group. Life was busy and I was learning. During this year of giving back to society I was told that as the president of North Shore Group I would get one thousand dollars to pay for my fare to the Australian Swap convention in Surfers Paradise. What a wonderful surprise, as I didn't know this when I said yes to being the president and life was handing me something good again . . . and I was wonderfully surprised and it felt great!

When I finished my year as the president, I again moved onto become an executive member of New Zealand Swap. This was another learning curve and another notch on my leadership belt.

Another experience was at three in the morning when a drunk driver missed the corner and crashed into the girls' bedroom at the front of the house. The car had broken the front steps and smashed a hole in the wall of the house. I was grateful they were staying at their fathers' that weekend. The crash had happened ten days before Christmas and the insurance company had everything repaired in time for our family Christmas party.

Playcentre started me on my journey to personal growth by teaching me about parenting and providing me with a thirst to learn. With my continued community night school classes I learned that I had low self-esteem and I had to educate myself to create happiness and success in my life.

One of the most interesting exercises was at a night course. We had to lie down and draw around the outline of each other's body then we had to find pictures and words in magazines that we liked and glue them onto our body shape.

After forty-five minutes, I had one of my legs with pictures of things I wanted in my home. My other leg had pictures of who I wanted to become as a person. One arm had places I wanted to travel and the other arm pictures of what I wanted for my work. Inside my stomach were pictures of things I loved and in my head was a collection of words that portrayed my present thoughts.

That exercise was the most positive and thought-provoking I have ever done. It helped my clarify ideas of who and what I wanted to become. Interestingly for me, once I saw the words I had pasted into my head image collage were all negative, this was one of my 'aha!'s' As a visual learner sighting proof about my thoughts something else made sense about my life – I had to change my thoughts. I kept that exercise for years as a guide to create the person I wanted to become. I used it as a guide to create my dreams. Words didn't work for me as well as the pictures. Later I learned was a personality trait.

I continued reading books and collecting articles in magazines, taking notes, attending free courses, listening to tapes and had a huge collection of information about who I was and what related to me. Over the years the only thing that changed was the words in my head.

Clearer but still confused with all the information I had collected, around the time of my fortieth birthday I decided I needed some clarification. I had information on:

- Stress because mine was always high

- Esteem because this had been low and I was constantly having to work on improving it

- Attitude because I had to keep working through negative vibes and concentrate on the positive things I was creating

- Communication because I had to rephrase my non verbal and verbal communication to positive

- Parenting because I had to continue learning about this role

- Careers because I had to rediscover what to do

- Soul because I searched for happiness and fulfillment

- Mind power because I learned about how I thought and could think

- Exercise because I worked on keeping myself motivated and physically fit

- Men because I tried to learn how to make a better choice next time

- My life purpose because I thought 'I must have one' and writing my life story message still intrigued me

- Time management because I was constantly juggling tasks and life
- Money because I was always stretched financially
- Positive quotes to read to keep my thoughts filled with positive ideas
- Poems to keep inspiring my thoughts
- Goals because I needed to learn to achieve more
- Business because I wanted to become successful
- Passions because I was re-learning what 'excited' me to include in my life
- Natural gifts because I was uncovering and developing the 'real me'
- Chakras because I was constantly working on aligning my body's energy
- Natural healing because I preferred these to other forms of medicine
- Past lives because I wondered about some of my experiences
- Being single because that was how I was living my life
- Star signs and birth dates for clues to myself
- Relationships so I could learn how to create a win/win relationships
- Religion and spirituality to learn about the voices and 'unusual' experiences I had
- Writing and more.

My quest for learning was constant. I had notes scribbled down from the library and the many borrowed books from friends. Some of the important lessons were from:

- Feel the Fear and Do it Anyway from Susan Jeffers
- Louise Hays books
- John Kehoe
- A collection of books by Richard Webster
- Stephen Covey and lots more

It was all good and positive. I loved it! This was in addition to the information I had learned and taught with the Playcentre leadership courses, which was absolutely fantastic as well. As I learned and achieved, another challenge and hurdle came my way . . . so another solution had to be found.

Consequently around the time of my 40th birthday, I was seeking more clarification; so one weekend I tacked all the information up on the wall of my bedroom. With a pen I systematically underlined all the words that were the same until I got some more ideas about myself. Words like leadership, spirituality and more were repetitive.

One book worked with my 'numbers' and I learned I was a 36/9 and this focused on my understanding my life purpose. Some of the experiences my soul apparently had to work on were: Expression and Sensitivity, Vision and Acceptance, Integrity and Wisdom. Then there was the Laws of Perfection, Honesty, Intuition, Flexibility Action and Higher Will. I recall thinking, "this is 'too much' and 'no wonder' I seem to always be having challenges!"

Humanitarism was a word that kept coming up especially with my birth numbers . . . and something that I didn't really want to own.

I was having enough challenges sorting out my own life, without wanting to be concerned that my life purpose was to be looking after others. I loved looking after my daughters but others . . . phew! At that stage in life at forty that was TOO daunting.

I tried meditation as a form of relaxation and 'getting in touch with my soul.' Even now I am still unable to master the techniques, instead I found Jeff Clarkson's soulful music and today continue to play his masterpiece "Butterfly" and other CD's.

Throughout the years inspiration songs were important to me with their message. My favorites are "Greatest Love of All" and "Search for the Hero," but many others have been sung and danced to on my journey.

During this time I learned I had gotten off track in my life during my teenage years. I had been a head prefect in primary school and also asked in Huntly High school, where I had said my first big 'NO' in life. As I delved back into my life, I realized that during those years, I was bullied at school and had lost my confidence and self-esteem and just wanted to hide at the back of the crowd. It was over a boy, (how unusual) and because another girl liked him, other girls verbally bullied me. Strange how this turn of events had a huge impact on my life.

I also learned that being born the third child and middle daughter, I never felt I had a special place. We had the eldest daughter and baby of the family and only boy, which meant these were special positions to have in a family and then there was me, the daughter in the middle. And somewhere in here, unknown to the family and even me, I became a peacemaker.

During that time in society, there was also the common phrase, "be seen and not heard," and so in reality that was how I was. I didn't really join in conversations and in hindsight realize I did not form opinions on matters either. Instead I just went with the flow with many situations. I don't recall being unhappy about it or even aware it was happening, so no gripes about it . . . it just is.

One of my many courses I attended in my early days was where someone commented I always had a smile on my face. They said, because of that it was impossible for people to read 'who' I was or even if it was the real me. They wondered what was I hiding and why I didn't show emotion and feelings. That was an eye-opener . . . and great feedback.

My underlying challenge was I had unconsciously developed low selfesteem. I didn't know so I couldn't do anything until I had diagnosed my problem. Only then I could start to consciously make changes because I knew what solutions I were needed.

From Playcentre to SWAP, I embraced every opportunity to learn and have new experiences. At my first Swap conference I heard about personality differences. I was sitting next to Ron my brother when we did the exercise and was amazed at the differences and clarification in people and also that we were both opposites. Things started to make more sense to me as to whom I was, and why I was different to other people and couldn't grasp certain skills (like managing money), and enjoyed teaching and happy to become a leader. This made sense to why my ex-husband drove me up the wall with his perfectionism in certain areas of his life.

The old saying, "when the student is ready the teacher arrives" rings true . . . I was beginning to understand!

Hindsight Insight

The concept behind the gratitude principal is the more we give to others, the more we are likely to receive. However, we also need to be in a position to give and it is not necessarily money. Giving your time and energy, is equally important. Sometimes we can give and other times we can't. Albeit when we give, we are often rewarded in different ways than we realize.

Recall moments in your life or analyze situations in your life now and count your gratitude blessings and thank those who are supporting you.

_____

_____

_____

_____

_____

_____

Educating yourself is your answer to fulfillment and happiness in life. Everyone has free will to follow this path and the universe never forces it upon you. However, if you keep getting stuck in similar situation in life, you either learn the lesson and make positive choices to move forward or for the rest of life you will be 'stuck in that rut.' Usually there are many 'out of the box' answers and ultimately if they have positive learning, they are helpful. If it supports your growth and provides unconditional love you are likely to be on track.

What are you needing answers for that you need to learn? Don't delay, as Nike says 'Just do it'.

_____

_____

_____

_____

_____

_____

Chapter 10

Sailing a Different Course

I must go down to the seas again, to the lonely sea and the sky
And all I ask is a tall ship and a star to steer her by.

—John Masefield

A sailor all my life, I found peace on the water with nature and the elements.

In the process of re-learning who I was, I was constantly out of my comfort zone trying something new. Activities that had brought me pleasure in my younger days were re-explored and one of them was sailing.

Growing up in small town had us involved in many community activities and sports. Dad had been a sailor for most of his life, and shared his passion with us. A group of local fathers had used their skills and spent a winter helping each other build the fleet of 'P Class' yachts for their children. Consequently, every Sunday afternoon our family would go sailing in the yachts they had built. We had meetings to learn sailing tactics and it was a fun family affair with social activities and sailing regattas.

I was never particularly good but I had learned the basics of sailing. When my next adventure started and the skipper had more faith in me that I had in myself, I learned I was a better sailor than I suspected.

When the girls were away for three weeks over the Christmas holidays, I did some work around the home and had time for myself.

One year I decided to go sailing. I had already been crew for some races and sailed on a friends boats but this time I decided to try something different.

I found a skipper who wanted an additional lady on the boat to sail with a couple and himself. I discussed the rules over the telephone and had a very long chat before I met him. It was during these chats that I learned a few months earlier, as weird as this sounds I had been 'underneath' his farm.

I had won a trip to the Lost World in Waitomo where I had the opportunity to learn how to abseil. To enter the Lost World, we had to abseil down three hundred feet into the valley in pairs. As I had gone on the trip on my own, I did not have a partner to share and a lady volunteered to join me. It was a fantastic experience abseiling down and I squealed words of delight as we descended. My partner said she enjoyed traveling down with me because of my excitement it made it more stimulating for her as we discussed the undergrowth and views on our journey. At the bottom we squeezed into wet suits and were given caver's helmets. Our ascent was via caves and climbing walls and swimming in the streams until we had scrambled back to the top of the valley.

It was an awesome experience and my first introduction to caving. Later that evening around six I started my drive home. The countryside was closing down for the day and a huge yellow moon was climbing over the distant hills and mist was spilling over the paddocks as stock settled in for the night. As I was driving I was listening to Elton John's music and a song about the big yellow moon rising above the hills started to play. It was eerie; living the experience of the song that suddenly played on the radio. It was a great finish to another new adventure.

During the telephone chats prior to my deciding to join the cruise, I learned some of the caves were under his farm. Albeit, when I eventually went to met Barry I found a grown man playing on his boat like it was his favorite toy. I later discovered many men, including my father enjoyed his boat like this.

Eventually my Christmas holiday started and the girls had gone away for three weeks with their dad for their holidays. Although I worried about them I was learning I had to 'chill out' myself.

I joined the boat laden down with a dozen bags, food and my gear.

I had been chilling a bottle of Diva sparking wine ready for my holiday. My adventure started as we motored out of Auckland harbor at dusk. We were cruising up to the Bay of Island and it was my first night sail. The wind was light and the sun was still shining as we left the confines of Pine Harbor. Once we had packed the final bags of gear below, I decided it was time to celebrate. Cruising past Waiheke and the outer islands, we could see twilight over Auckland City. The lights sparked and then twinkled as we moved further afield. I shared my bubbly with the crew and, we had Joshua Kadison music blaring from the stereo as we sailed north. Sitting at the back of the boat, soaking in the perfect scene, I experienced a sense of peace and bliss.

I felt safe with the skipper, which I think is an important aspect of sailing. Some skippers are reckless sailors; this one erred on caution, which is important on the sea. With a calm sea our trip was smooth The dusk gave way to the night sky and stars began twinkling Out on the water it was interesting learning about the navigational lights on the charts and then searching for them on the water. Because the winds were light the skipper decided to motor and set a straight course north rather then tack with the wind. It was still fabulous being at one with the sea with the gentle putt putt of the motor pushing us forward.

I had never met the other couple so after sharing a dinner sitting out the back of the boat, we sat chatting the rest of the evening. It was wonderful to be with adult company, interesting people and on the sea enjoying an adventure. The moon rose in the sky and shone its bright light out onto the water, causing it to shimmer almost providing a light line to follow to the horizon. Peace pervaded me in the warm summer night me on the water. I decided I must have been a pirate in my past life . . . or sailed the seven seas of the world, to feel so relaxed and content on the sea!

We were on allotted shifts for the night. I gave everyone a hug and found my bunk downstairs. The two of us with boating experience were allotted shifts. The skipper decided to stay up all night with the other chap keeping awake with him until three the next morning. Supposedly they would wake me for my watch so I could keep him awake and provide the cups of tea and chatting. However it wasn't until four o'clock that I was woken with a jolt.

Neither of the men had been tired so they had decided to let me sleep. However when a pod of dolphins joined the yacht, swimming around the hull and diving under the back of the boat, they knew it would be something new for me. And it was! It was difficult to see the shapes of the dolphin's bodies as they skimmed through the water. Their movement caused fluorescent bubbles to form in the water and float to the surface. They darted and dived around us for about ten minutes before disappearing off into the dark waters of the sea. I decided it could be a good sign of magical times ahead to experience such a wonderful display of nature. Like this poem:

Only the Moon Knows

Colours spread across the sky

The sun goes down

The moon stands high

Shining rays, they disappear

As dolphins leap into the air

Only the glisten

Of the moon's dim light

Is there to guide them through the night

A peaceful creature

Harmless and free

Ruler of the ocean Friend of the sea

When the morning comes they can't be seen

Only the moon knows, Dolphins have been.

Kirsty Wilson

Over the next few days I found a new *me* again . . . the ocean, the wind, music, companionship and a new enjoyment in life. Once again I was in a different space as I rediscovered myself. Then while at peace something new happened I had never experienced.

The words just started coming . . . they scrambled into my mind, continuous and never ending, until I decided the only way to get rid of them and stop them was to write them on paper. And so I started! They made sense but didn't quite make sense. From the words I jotted down I created a poem . . . after poem . . . after poem. I wasn't sure where they came from, but the words were very real and I began to carry a notebook with me all the time.

My favorite time was at dawn. I would sneak out of bed, dress myself with whatever warm wet weather gear was close, tip toe to the back of the boat, climb into the dinghy and quietly push myself away from the yacht. Once I drifted away from the boat, I would row out to a quiet place and enjoy the solitude and peace of the early morning. Fish would jump, dropping goblets of water onto the calm seas that would sprinkle like diamonds in the morning sun and spread ripples across the surface. This was a place where I discovered peace and oneness with the universe. I floated around or sometimes found a beach for a dawn walk. Having the world to myself at this time of day was a treasure I had never experienced. Everything was new and crisp in the morning air as the day began. After an hour or two I would return about 7.30am for a morning cup of tea with the skipper and crew.

Over the ten-day holiday I wrote many poems that flowed to me. Some arrived the same way; scrambling into my thoughts and others more sedately. They were all about the sea and fun experiences of being out on the sea. Some were whimsical and others were more serious.

I didn't know why I was experiencing this and I thought maybe they were channeled. I wasn't thinking them they just started to bubble in my brain and continue to repeat until I wrote them down. Sometimes I had to write very quickly as the words would come so rapidly. Other times, I would just get a line or two.

Once back on land a few poems continued to flow. Eventually, I decided to combine these, along with quotes and snippets of historical in formation into my first book, titled *Sailing a Different Course*. When it was compiled into a big folder, I had it sitting on my ironing board when I suddenly burst into tears. I realized, this was another new experience as I was and sharing my ideas and thoughts with the world and opening myself up for praise and criticism. I self-published the book, marketed it, had book reviews and sold a few copies. I didn't cover my costs, nevertheless, it was an experience – and I thought maybe the answer to my first haunting message, *"write your life story."*

Later I realized how important those life-changing thoughts were when someone criticized my poems. I knew they weren't Robert Burns or anything fantastic. I decided critics are the people that haven't got the guts to 'do it themselves.' I have learned the lessons about critics in life. There are always lots of them, they don't like change or have the courage to put themselves out on a limb.

I'll never know exactly where or who the poems came from. In hindsight, maybe it was my grandmother or some other soul from my past life or one of my learning experiences I needed in training for the 'big day' – whatever that was going to be!

Almost every other weekend for the next five years while they girls were away I sailed with Barry, exploring the bays and seas of the Hauraki Gulf. He said there were two people he felt safe enough to sail his boat while he went below to sleep. One was his mate who was an old 'sea dog' and the other was me; because if there was something I didn't know I would ask rather than think I could handle it myself.

One day sailing back into Gulf Harbor I had an unusual experience. It was a beautiful perfect day for sailing and Barry was down below snoozing. The boat, wind, sail was aligned in what I've heard sailors call in 'the grove' when you hardly have to steer the boat instead it almost steers itself. The yacht was sailing beautifully with the sails full, the slap of the waves on the side of the yacht and the seas sparkling like diamonds.

There was no warning when it happened. In a nanosecond it was like a flash! I was catapulted into a realm that somehow appeared above the earth. It was like a split second cosmic style experience. It was a weird experience and as I tried to analyze it, I couldn't find an answer. Years later, I have never again experienced anything similar.

Maybe these were lessons I needed in life to learn to sail my own course.

Hindsight Insight

When you are enthusiastic and enjoying life your body's energy level changes. Endorphins are released into your body and you enjoy the

'feel good' experience. Additionally, engaging in activities you enjoy or are passionate about is when you are likely to meet other people with the same thinking and enthusiasm towards life and where you are likely to meet new friendships.

If you want to 'feel good' 24/7, include more of your interests and passions into your life? What do you need to include?

_____

_____

_____

_____

_____

_____

'Learn to Be Still' is a song The Eagles sing. It is in the meditative state that we are likely to receive 'inside' information flow into our minds, which will help us on our life journey. This time can be a time of day-dreaming, beach walking, or any activity that provides you an opportunity to soul search and listen to any incoming messages and/ or appreciate a quiet time in your life. It can also be a time before you have fallen asleep or fully awake in the morning. Become consciously aware of this time and 'listen' for the messages that will support you and your growth. Ignore any negative ones.

Are you providing time for soul searching in your life? If not, turn off the television and contemplate for ten or fifteen minutes to start your processes.

_____

_____

_____

_____

Chapter 11

Spirit World Intervention

I am a radiating center of divine love, mighty to
attract my good and to radiate good to others.

—Daily Word

It was the late 1980's. My bedroom was at the back of the house with a walk through wardrobe into the bedroom. Ever since I first became a mother, I had rarely slept through the night. Apparently, it's normal, but I always felt 'linked' and would wake just before they called out. OR . . . was it their calling waking me. Of course I didn't know, but waking through the night for me was normal. This was my first 'haunting' experience in the house.

From a deep sleep, I sat upright in bed A male voice was booming out to me . . .

WRITE YOUR LIFE STORY.

It was very clear and only said those four words I looked at my digital clock that shone in the dark It was exactly 3.00am. I wondered - Who was there and who spoke to me? Tentatively I turned on the light. The room was empty. I checked the girls and house, turning on all the outside lights. I found nothing. I lay awake for a while . . . perplexed . . . deep in thought. Eventually, I snuggled up and went back to sleep – with the lights still on. I was puzzled. I had NO idea who or what it was.

Over the years, I have wondered what that message was about.

Later I learned that three in the morning was a very spiritual time, and I still wonder who that message was from and I can still recall the voice.

At that stage I had not written any articles or books and was not interested in writing. A few years later, I had an urge to start.

I thought I would write a book about maintaining a positive attitude. I was continually working on, keeping my thoughts positive and learning 'this skill' as I wanted to achieve more success and was on a continuous learning curve.

Instead I wrote a book about single parenting. I would write at five o'clock in the morning before the girls were out of bed and at night when they were in bed. I sought advice from a writer as a mentor. Afterwards I thought maybe that was the message, "WRITE YOUR LIFE STORY."

Since then I have written numerous small books, articles and eBooks, each one of them writing more of my life story. This book, twenty years later, is the culmination story of my life and finally I assume this IS the book I was destined to write.

Strange things happened and in hindsight they are being answered. We had an episode where Kirsty was accused of hiding cards from a packet of potato chips that belonged to someone else. I searched the house and questioned her. She was adamant that she didn't touch the cards.

In reality I couldn't see why she would be interested in these cards from a packet of potato chips. However, apparently, they were a collector's item for kids at school and swapping and sharing was a popular event during school lunchtimes. The people were insistent she had taken them while Kirsty was adamant she had not.

In the midst of this someone suggested that I write a letter to Kirsty's angels. This was my first introduction to 'angels' and I didn't know what to expect. In the letter I asked for guidance and help for Kirsty about the situation and I placed it under my mattress.

When she came home from school that day, she said she had to make a telephone call. Immediately she rang the person and with the wisdom of a forty-year-old and in a different, mature woman's voice she told them, "I did not take the cards."

I'm sure they didn't believe her, but as soon as she had spoken to them she returned back to her normal self and voice. Years later we discovered what had happened and Kirsty had been the scapegoat.

I was amazed at the experience I just witnessed. For just a few moments Kirsty had taken on the demeanor of an adult. I told her I was proud of her and she replied nonchalantly, "Well I didn't take the cards, so now they know."

This was my first experience with writing to angels and I decided I would try it again if needed in my life. I didn't make a conscious decision that I would be open minded to experiences from the spirit world, but as normal when something unusual happened I went in search of answers.

One morning when I woke at five as usual I had a message constantly repeating in my head.

Tell her I love her and want her to be happy.

This didn't make any sense to me I wondered what was happening to me this time. I didn't know who it was and whom it was for. I racked my mind for an answer. I worked my way through a list of possibilities of 'who' the 'her' could be. Then who would want the message repeated . . . I love her . . . and why would he want her to be happy.

By about seven-thirty, I realized who the message was for.

The previous day I had visited a girlfriend's house that she was moving from. She had lived there with her partner who had died seven years earlier. I decided he had channeled this message to me (if that was the correct terminology), and wanted me to pass his message on to her before she left the house they had shared.

I tried to phone her at home before I left home for work. There was no reply. Finally at around ten-thirty during my morning teatime break at work I got her on the telephone.

"This is weird," I said. "I have never had anything happen to me like this before, but I think I have had a message from Graham for you."

"That's weird too," she replied. "I think he visited me last night."
"Graham told me to tell you that 'he loved you and it was time to move on,'" I said.

And, I told her about the words that woke me and continued to repeat in my mind and I suspected they were from Graham for her. I could think of no one else I knew that this message related to. And so, I passed on the message, "Graham loved you and wants you to move on in life and be happy."

As I spoke the words to her, my whole body started to tingle. It was like I had pins and needles from my head to toes. My hands were shaking and as I left the office where I made the telephone call, I was still tingling. It took me forty-five minutes before my fingers returned to normal and I could type on my computer.

I felt light and airy . . . and weird but happy. I had obviously done my good deed for the day!

I still felt something was holding me back in life. I could not pin point what it was exactly. There was a constant reminder that the house was not mine. I cannot blame the girls as they were only repeating what they were told.

Over the years I had nourished the mandarin and grapefruit trees with grass clippings around the roots, and each year we had lovely fruit.

I would tease the girls about how I was a good gardener (it was sheer luck and I just did what Mum told me as she had the green fingers). Anyway, they would always come back with an answer that their father had told them, that he had planted the trees and the only reason they were any good was because he had planted them. In fact he had, but it was ten years ago.

Another time, I would comment about the sunshine coming into the house. It was bright and sunny and they would remind me (words from their father) that he had built it. Of course he had, but somehow even though I had brought the house of him, laid the concrete paths, Dad and I had put up some fences, I had laid the second hand carpet and paid all the bills and maintained it, and he was still telling them it was his house. He was also telling them, I was his wife until 'death do us part' so I do not blame the girls for any of their comments.

I tried to make life easy for them with visiting him and his influence. However, this negative energy was always around and started to affect me. In reality it was not but it was an indication that I needed to 'do' or 'think' differently. It was time for more growth.

I had learned through my many courses and books, that investing in me was the only path for my success. Over the years I had been babysitting children before they went to school and had cleaning jobs and had sold my small business Funtasia Fashions, so I had a few dollars in the bank.

Rather than paying off the mortgage I decided the best way was to continue on my journey of personal development. John Kehoe, a Canadian motivational speaker and workshop leader, was speaking at SWAP; the business group I belonged to was visiting New Zealand. I went to the freebies and then enrolled in the course with my hard earned three hundred and forty five dollars. I was seriously searching for an answer.

My expectations were open. In one of the meetings we were asked to invite people who were causing us challenges. As an effort to im prove the relationship I asked William. In very colorful language, he said, "NO."

On Sunday night the course finished and although I had learned new ideas, no real answer had emerged. I was disappointed and felt like I had wasted my hard-earned dollars.

On Tuesday morning after the girls had gone to school I took the garbage outside and was putting it into the bag to take out to the roadside for collection it happened!

The voice was very clear. It was a male voice, not loud but in a moderate medium tone and it just said.

Buy a house and income.

It was not a glamorous time to get such an important message, but clear as a bell, it spoke in my mind. NEVER would I have thought of that. I decided it was the answer I was looking for! Sell this house that William had built and buy a house where I could earn some income from a tenant. It was a fantastic idea!

The voice and message in my head was so vivid and clear and only included those words. I had learned enough to know after my books and courses that the unexpected was an answer coming from the 'ether' or 'universe,' although I had not quite formed my opinion on that.

I had started attending a church called Unity, where they teach you 'how to think' rather than 'what to think,' and this philosophy felt okay to me. I had not read the Bible but still felt a connection. It was about thinking positive, good values, working through your challenges, learning on your journey, looking after and loving yourself, forgiving yourself and helping others and mankind. It was a kindred philosophy to what I was learning through my journey of personal development.

Anyway, back to the home and income, I started searching the local papers that same day. A few people thought I was a bit crazy, I didn't tell them how I got the message, but they could see some sense in my decision, so things started to roll along slowly.

I visited some of the local real estate agents and was told of my ideal house. After visiting the street I could not find the sign but found another house for sale, which I didn't like. It was May, six weeks after I had attended the John Kehoe course.

Over the next few months I continued searching and put my house on the market as well. Finally, the agent came back to me and said, "Janice, I don't know why you don't like that house, it has got exactly what you tell me you are looking for." So, I agreed to go and take another look with him. As luck would have it, he took me and we went to a different house in the street from which I had seen earlier.

Immediately I understood what he meant. It had everything I wanted. Without hesitation I put in an offer. He said his wife was bringing someone to look through it after me who also put in an offer.

With my offer submitted, the owner was having both presented to her in a few days. I waited with baited breathe at ten o'clock two days later to hear the verdict. The telephone came during my lunch-time break; only to be told both offers were exactly the same and we both had to resubmit new offers.

My mortgage was pre-approved so I called my mortgage broker to ask if I could afford another five thousand. She suggested I offer $5,500. When the offers were resubmitted, it was my additional five hundred that bought me the house.

Elated, I called her and asked why she had suggested the additional money.

"It just popped into my head," she said.

And so, my new home and income was now reality. I was getting used to these ideas from the 'ether' universe or whoever . . . so understood that this was the new house for my girls and myself.

The day I moved was like a big party as family and friends arrived to help. Mum spent the morning in the Flanshaw Road kitchen, making morning teas and lunches. In the afternoon she moved to the new house in Cron Avenue kitchen for afternoon tea, followed by champagne and appetizers as the move was completed.

And so one door closed and one part of my life finished, and another chapter was opening and whole new exciting unknown volume was beginning.

Hindsight Insight

Unexplainable situations have been described for hundreds of years in the bible and hundreds of other books, television programs and movies. Only one answer seemed to make any sense and that was the spirit world was real. These were my first real encounters and I was forced to expand my thinking because of these experiences I had.

What unexplainable situations have you experienced that were opportunities for you to embrace some new thoughts? Do you need to reexamine them?

_____

_____

_____

_____

_____

_____

Trusting your instincts is another skill that you need to learn. Often you don't want to but within you, your inner compass, spirit or soul or whatever you wish to call it, is urging you in another direction in life. Negative energy will always hold you back until you find solutions. If you want to move forward in life then it is time to open your mind to new ideas.

What negative energy situations have you experienced that you may still need to resolve?

_____

_____

_____

_____

_____

_____

Chapter 12

Abnormally Haunted

Life is the movie you see through your own unique eyes.
It makes little difference what's happening out there.
It's how you take it that counts.

—Denis Waitley

I had no idea of the adventure ahead when I moved into this house. It is hard to describe the era of the house but it was wood and built in the 1960's. It was painted brown and surrounded by mature trees. From the road, it had a long driveway that dipped slowly down a small hill and then up a steep grade up the other side. At the top it leveled out into a flat area for turning into a double carport, or you could drive straight ahead for parking for the outside unit.

In the carport was a mechanic's pit, which was covered with two inch thick planks of wood about twelve inches wide. These slotted together to cover up the pit, which was about five feet deep with concrete stairs at one end. I made a rule with the girls that these pieces of wood were never to be removed. As luck would have it, or 'unlucky' for me, one day the girls cleaned out the mechanical rubbish and made a hut down in there while I was out. Unfortunately although they put the wood back it had not slotted in properly.

The angle of the driveway meant I could not see the wood when I drove up onto and into the carport. The day the wood was not replaced correctly and the front drivers' side wheel of the car ended up falling into the hole. I suspected what had happened as the front of the car dropped down. When I got out of the car, I wondered how I would get the car back onto the level. Luckily for the girls, they had both gone out and did not bear the brunt of my anger.

I had joined the Automobile Association when Kirsty was born and I telephoned for help. They were interested and amused in my dilemma. The car was jacked up to raise the front wheel. The slab of wood was replaced properly under the tire and the car was let down back on to the correctly placed plank of wood. It never happened again.

Once parked in the double carport, there was a long rectangular room in front of it that the original owner had used as storage and outside garden shed. Later I converted this into an outside bedroom with a mezzanine floor.

From the carport a path ran along the side of the house with a thirty-foot Rimu tree beside it. You walked past the main bedroom into a small private courtyard. This had a six-foot fence, with a fifteen-foot tulip tree in the corner. It was paved with a fern garden along one side. At the end of the courtyard you stepped up onto a wooden deck with a fifty-foot jacaranda tree in the middle it. A conservatory opened off onto this.

The inside décor of the house was cream with brown exposed beams, cream shag carpet and wooden framed windows, which was popular with houses in the 1960's. My main bedroom received the morning sun and had a scenic outlook into the garden and trees. The girls' bedrooms were painted pale blue with Kirsty having the larger of the two rooms.

When I first went to view the house and entered the front doorway, the tenant had a painting of herself hung on the wall. She was dressed in an old-fashioned style costume with a long black cloak. It reminded me of Joan of Ark. She had an old fashioned gardening tool in her hand as a walking stick.

In the main bedroom she had another portrait. This time she was lounging in an old-fashioned sofa. She was wearing a long white princess style gown, looking very mysterious. She looked a very interesting lady with her jet-black hair, pale skin and bright red lipstick.

I was later to learn about her 'interesting' time in the house as well. The house sat elongated on the section. It had wooden paned windows that looked into the courtyard and out onto the peaceful green tree lined back yard. On one side was planted exotic trees, loquats and guavas and other fruit trees.

An outside unit was a new addition to the house and had been designed to match the 1960's style. The interior of this unit consisted of one large room and with a kitchenette in the corner and a shower and toilet. The previous owner had used the unit for counseling her clients.

One of my first jobs was to convert the outside studio into a rental unit and get tenants. Andy and his girlfriend became the first tenants. We heard later that a family member had originally owned this piece of land when it was an orchard.

For the first few months, Leila had difficulty sleeping in her room. Almost every night she would come into my bed in the early hours of the morning, telling me Trolls were waking her and talking to her. She was scared so would climb in with me for the rest of the night. Initially, I didn't think too much of this except she was dreaming and blaming her toys. The girls had gone through a stage of Troll toys when they were popular, and had a small collection of them. In an attempt to break the habit of the midnight escapes, I moved them out of her room. The problem continued. Eventually we found an answer and mastered the situation . . . or so it seemed.

Within a few months I also turned the outside storage room by the carport into a room by building in a mezzanine floor, getting steps up onto it and painting and carpeting the room. Again it was decked out in cream and my first thoughts were I would use it for an office for my coaching. After a few months this didn't work out so Kirsty move out there and Leila moved into her larger room inside and I had the smaller inside room as my office.

Kirsty loved her room and with her artistic talent started decorating it. She started with Celtic writing up the side of the stairs. It moved onto the shelves, windowsills and pieces of furniture. I thought while she was busy following her passion she wasn't getting into mischief.

I was still surprised when I went home one day to find all the cushions removed off my lounge suite. I went searching. I found Kirsty had taken them up onto the mezzanine floor where she slept. They were on top of each other and she was able to lie on her back and paint the roof. She had already painted whales and dolphins on the walls and now was painting a fairy scene. It was fantastic.

It was déjà vu. When I was her age I painted my bedroom pink and green striped and spotted walls. When Kirsty had finished her paintings, there were fabulous and I regret not taking any photos.

After a few months, we went away for the weekend and I left the keys so Andy and Shelley could use my laundry inside the house. They had become good friends with the girls and it was a big happy family. When I arrived home one Sunday night, Andy met me with a sorrowful tale.

He had parked his four-wheel drive van in the normal place on the flat parking area outside the unit. They had gone into the laundry to start the washing when they had heard a huge crash. They ran outside to see what had happened and the van had rolled down the driveway. It had gone through the neighbors' fence and collided with the BMW car parked below.

After the accident, he had spoken to the neighbors and then drove the van back up the hill. He had stopped and tested the brakes half way up the hill and they had worked perfectly. He was adamant that the brakes didn't fail and convinced that something had pushed it down the driveway. I listened with my mind whirling; this was new to me! Something pushed his huge vehicle down the drive.

They were too scared to come into the house and the washing from Saturday was still in the machine. This was weird!

I also went to speak to my neighbors and shared what Andy had told me. His parked van somehow ran down the driveway and although it was bizarre, it appeared to have been pushed. It was unexplainable. They turned to me, unperplexed and said, "YOU know the house is haunted!"

I was stunned, opened and closed my mouth a few times, and of course my answer was, "Well . . . no . . . I didn't!"

"It has been for years," they said.

Now I was learning! I had never experienced anything like this before!

Hindsight Insight

Often you are exposed to ideas from your children that are unusual or as adults you forget. You may have an answer, which may be also be different. As a parent, I have encouraged and ensured that I listened to them. You show respect and value to your children when you take time to hear their concerns. If you want to communicate with them when they are teenagers, you must encourage this from childhood.

Take note of yourself when you are having a conversation. Are you really listening or are you always ready to give your answer? Are you honoring the people who are communicating with you and do you need to make any changes?

_____

_____

_____

_____

_____

_____

Television programs portray some of these 'out of the world' experiences. I recall seeing one with Michael Jackson dancing after he had passed away and left our physical world. If my experiences had not happened to me, I would be a skeptic. I did have my ideas catapulted into another realm. It takes courage and insight to share these concepts with the world because you will be viewed differently. However that is the complexity of being human . . . we are all unique beings and fully entitled to share with the world. There will always be critics, who have nothing else to do except criticize others lives without having the confidence to examine their own.

Experiences in life are for us to learn . . . what experiences do you need to rethink or act upon?

_____

_____

_____

_____

_____

_____

Chapter 13

Normality – whatever that is

There are two days we should not worry about Yesterday, with its mistakes and heartaches. They are gone forever. Tomorrow is the other day. It has problems and possibilities, but until the sun rises, it is unborn and unreal. Today is the only day left. Anyone can fight a battle for just one day. Only when we add the burdens of those other two days are we likely to fail.

—Unknown

As I journeyed through life's ups and downs in Cron Ave, I learned some valuable lessons about myself and how to think. I was always out of my comfort zone learning something new as I searched for answers, therefore always a chance of mistakes.

After all the bills were paid, I never had any money spare for extras. The girls had to work and earn it themselves which taught them great working ethics. I became the taxi; running them to and from their jobs. Mobile phones became the 'in' thing and with their after-school and weekend work they were able to purchase one for themselves.

During these last few years at Cron, they both experienced episodes of bullying. I took both episodes seriously as they needed positive solutions.

When Leila started to get bullied with death threats in text messages we tried matching phone numbers and then took her telephone to the police. They called the number and discovered it was a girl from

school, using her brother's mobile phone so she would be undetected. A chat from the police with the girl and her parent's and
Leila never received any again.

At Kirsty's school a group of girls ganged up against her after
dating someone's ex-boyfriend. She had ditched school for three
weeks before I learned about it. Eventually, in tears, she refused to
go back. It was early in the year and I wanted a solution other than
her leave school. I had just purchased her sixth form uniform and
money was tight but I knew she had to change schools.

She was a top scholar with art and math her best subjects. I found
a school that she could transfer to and she moved to Waitakere
College. The curriculum had been taught in reverse sequence from
Rutherford, however she continued to excel in her art and by the
time she left in the seventh form, was the top art student.

During the girls' experiences Leila would talk with me more than
Kirsty. This was a personality trait and as I guided Leila, I would
often hear her on the phone helping her friends with the same advice
I had given her. It was wonderful to hear her pass on the ideas and
learn from her experiences.

A few years later, a primary school friend commented to Leila how
she worked through every challenge positively and moved forward
in life. Apparently Leila's reply was because her mum had helped
her. That was lovely to hear. As a parent everything I learned I tried
to teach the girls. In our busy life today, many parents do not learn
themselves therefore unable to pass on wisdom to their children. I
always did the best that I could.

One of Kirsty's friends became her boyfriend and it was a major
decision when she asked if he could rent our studio. My sisters were
coming to stay during the school holidays and it took a few bottles
of wine over dinner for us to make a decision. We agreed and he
moved in.

He really was an asset to our family and became like a brother to
Laura. I coached him in his career choices and introduced him to
our music sessions on the piano. He started to learn the guitar and
he told us his grandfather had played in Joe Cocker's band.

While he lived in the studio, we had more teenagers visit our home
and my philosophy was that I knew where the girls were. One boy
who was about six-feet tall and always wore a beanie continued to

come inside to use the toilet. I asked him why he didn't use the toilet in the unit. He remarked he wanted to read the positive quotes I displayed on my inside toilet wall. I was pleased and astounded.

When the girls were younger, I had decided to take every chance to educate them with positive personal growth information. They wouldn't always listen to me (typical teenagers) so I had a corkboard on the toilet wall and displayed positive quotes and motivational poems on it. I also had a collection of my Unity Daily Word inspirational books. I could tell someone had been reading them, because they were never left as tidy. Albeit, it was great to hear that not only my girls but also others were reading all the positive information as well. Yeah! It was working!

Kirsty and her boyfriend wanted to live together. Kirsty asked for help with the deposit and because Leila wanted to move in with them I agreed. At the last minute Kirsty told me it was only her and not Leila with them, and I refused to pay it. That caused an uproar and we had our first major upheaval and family disputes.

They moved in with my first tenant. Later, Kirsty told me they had eaten McDonalds for six months. I knew she could cook so it wasn't my problem. At least they were eating.

After seven years working as a travel tutor I had only received two dollars an hour pay increase. Changes had happened on campus and I had to travel further to a new campus and pay huge parking fees. I was still classified as a part time worker because I had the holidays off to look after the girls rather than them become 'home alone' children who inevitably got into mischief.

I enjoyed the workplace benefits. As part of the course the students had educational sightseeing tours around New Zealand. On one of them I was taking a group to the South Island. The day prior to leaving, a student had to return home to her sick father. It was decided my Mum Jean, could join us.

We were in Nelson having dinner when a stranger overheard Mum and I and joined our conversation. He told us one of his coworkers was the new staff member who would be joining me at work. No one liked him and customers complained about him and they were pleased he was leaving their employment. I thought that was unusual, until I met him!

We didn't work in the department so I did not have much contact with him. When I was appointed the new tourism tutor instead of him, he became the dragon his previous coworker mentioned! It had taken six months before he vented his anger on me.

We had a work rule to never search through one another's desk when we needed information about one of their students in their earlier study. We were always busy and often left notes for each other instead.

As I was new in my role as tourism tutor I asked my manager before I left a note on the dragon man's desk. We had an open plan office and our desks now faced each other. When he arrived at his desk and saw the note, he looked up and glared at me. I felt knives shooting through the air at me! He stormed over to the manager, interrupted her conversation with a student and asked if he needed to find the information about his former students. Of course she said yes. He glared at me again, before storming out of our office. The doors swung on the hinges as he to stamped his way towards our archives room. I guessed the information was still in a box next to his desk but I daren't tell him.

A few minutes later we heard his return. The other tutors and I glanced at each other and smirking, quickly buried ourselves in our work. The door was shoved open almost coming off the hinges. He stormed to his desk, rumbled through his papers and found the information about his student that I needed. Then he came and stood over me while I was sitting at my desk and let his anger rip. He was over six feet tall with a red face that shone like a fire engine and had slick back hair, like they wore in the 1930's. He told me he was angry because he should have got the new job instead of me. He was angry because of a dozen other reasons, and no matter what I said he yelled and performed like a two-year-old child having a tantrum. A few minutes later he finished and stormed out of the office again.

I had never experienced such rage and childish like tantrum behavior from an adult. Everyone in the office was shocked and horrified and asked how I was. My hands were shaking and my legs felt like they had turned to jelly. I couldn't stand up. I told them he was being a bully, which we already surmised because of the stories we were hearing about him in his classroom and students in tears, and how he spoke to his wife on the telephone. I called the head of the department, explained what happened and asked if I could go home. He replied, "yes, and take the rest of the week off." I said I didn't need to and would return to work the next day.

My years of my personal development gave me the knowledge so I analyzed my experience. He was a bully and I was his victim, so he thought. However, because I understood Transactional Analysis after my bullying at school and marriage, I knew the symptoms and the solutions. He was trying to blame me for his problems, insecurities and vent his anger on me. Although I was the target I didn't believe the insults he yelled at me. Although I was understandably upset, I communicated back to him assertively and my self-esteem was still intact. These were my solutions.

Also, I realized if I had experienced this workplace bullying, fifteen years earlier I would have fallen back into the victim role of my earlier life. Our workplace relationship would have reverted into a lose/lose level. However, because I had educated myself with years of personal development, I was now wiser and understood the situation. I wasn't part of the problem if it hadn't been me, it would have been someone else he abused. I was astute enough now to realize it was a lose/win situation. He was the loser and I was the winner.

Our head of department had told me we needed to discuss it and become friends! I refused and said I would only talk to the dragon in his office with him present. I was concerned about another onslaught of his anger.

Four days later he arrived back at work. Consequently, we meet in the boss's office at ten o'clock on Friday morning. Our boss suggested we talk it over during lunch and again told to become friends. He continued that we were both divorced, had two young daughters and many other similarities to chat about.

I said one of the most important 'no's' in my life. I told the boss that I would discuss work only and not become friends.

I was not going to be drawn back into a lose/lose relationship with the dragon. With my newfound confidence after my personal development training I had set new rules for my life. I only wanted good relationships and create win/win relationships. I knew what I was aiming for and who I wanted in my life.

During the week I had told my mother about the episode at work and she suggested I put standard roses around my desk to protect myself from his negative energy. I loved the humor of that idea, but instead purchased four small lavender plants that I strategically placed on my desk along with more positive quotes.

We continued working together for about a month before he left. One year later I understood those first remarks made about him by his ex-colleagues and the reason why no one liked him. He went roaming into another workplace causing chaos.

By this stage in my life I was exhausted after fifteen years as a single mum, working and parenting. Every holiday I became sick as my body collapsed from exhaustion. I pushed myself, only relaxing when I was shattered and collapsed to watch a video.

Also the girls' father had attempted to receive maintenance money from me via social security for having the girls in the weekends. I was not very happy! He was not working and on a benefit after a sup posed accident at work and was trying to get ME to pay money to him as well.

During this time I went to a Robert Kiyosaki presentation. I had read his books and started looking for a rental property, using the equity I had in Cron as a deposit. I decided on my suburb and it took me six months to find a unit. I purchased it within twenty-four hours. Within ten days it was rented and I became a landlord. I felt like I was moving forward financially and starting to succeed.

I left my job and decided I would become a life coach, as I physically couldn't continue living with the stress from work and running the home and family. Something had to change and it was my thoughts and actions. In the end this decision was good for my health but bad for my finances.

Once Kirsty had moved out I had international students from work live with us and this supplemented my finances. Some of them were easy and others were tricky especially the Chinese as they were used to being the only child and now were living as part of a family.

Over the years the girls had continued to visit their father every second weekend. He would collect and drop them off in his old yellow station wagon. When he walked past me he refused to make eye contact or talk but I didn't leave their bags at the door now as I felt safer and there were always people around. He was still an odd man.

As the girls grew older they refused to visit him and he blamed it on me. He had gone on ACC for a neck injury and had not worked for years. Even the girls had tried to find him a job but to no avail. He decided to return to Perth to live. They chose not to say good-bye to him. I assumed something had happened which they wouldn't tell me.

Mum and Dad continued to visit. Dad always brought his box of tools and Mum some home baking. The tradition from my teen-age years of 'cocktail' singing with Dad continued and we would gather around the piano with Dad on his mouthorgan while mum prepared tea.

Later my niece came and stayed with us. She was bright and bubbly and a breath of fresh air in the family. She started teaching at a local country school and would leave for school in bare feet even on the winter early mornings. She introduced me to a book about past lives and it opened my eyes to another new way of thinking. She had recently returned from Jamaica and danced and moved like the Jamaicans when she listened to Bob Marley music. We decided that in her past life, she must have been a Jamaican nanny who walked bare footed and loved looking after children.

Once I met Kerry he came and went in and out of my life for a few months. He enjoyed the madness of my busy home and loved cooking us family barbeques in our courtyard under the jacaranda tree. One night while we had a barbeque we had an interesting experience as a small white owl came and sat in the tree and watched us. It was a spooky and eerie experience and I still wonder about its significance.

We split up for a few months but kept in touch. He was confused about his direction in life. I offered to coach him and lend him books but he refused my offer. He had other things he wanted to explore.

He had a wonderful sense of humor and sometimes whacky outlook on life. His family was very different from mine, whereas we created mutually rewarding relationships, they didn't. There was a lot of game playing and bullying tactics. He liked to do the right thing and more often than not this was at his expense of time and money that the family expected from him. My family worked together helping each other, whereas in his family it was different and seemed a one-way relationship with him always giving.

Occasionally, we met for a coffee, a kiss and cuddle but it would take me three days to return to normal. I decided that wasn't doing me any good and it was time to "let him go" as the universe says, and find someone who wanted to be with me. I had no sooner made the decision to do just that when he called and started quizzing me about who I was dating. At this stage I told him that it was none of his business, but we decided to meet to get my books back. Stranger than fiction, we got back together and are still hanging in there. Not without a learning curve on the journey!

Finally, with the girls on their journeys and me still working and no one to help with housework and gardening, I was exhausted again. I had three tenants but not going forward in life. With my finances a mess again and not making the money from my coaching, although I was doing some part time work, I decided to sell Cron Ave and downsize to my apartment.

During these years I had learned about my personality. I was an entrepreneur, ideas, and creative, always starting never finishing, lousy with money, emotive, leader, teacher, fun, think outside the box type of person. I made my decisions on emotion rather than logic. When I had learned this I was a much happier person with who I was. Even today I am living up to my uniqueness and do not compare myself with other people and my esteem is much higher. Thus making the choice to move was in fact another journey in life.

It was an interesting experience as I prepared the house for sale. I had lots of furniture to dispose of and the house needed a few paint jobs and tidying up. My tomboy skills from my youth once again came into use.

One of my last experiences with one of 'my spiritual visitor's' was when I had a real estate agent visit. While we were chatting at the front door, my lounge room door handle turned, the door opened half way for a few seconds and then closed. There was no logical reason, no wind and no slamming. I had just re-varnished my entrance floor and had a sense that someone came to look and check out the real estate agent. A lady had just passed away at my church and I felt that she was now there guarding over the house. It felt left in good hands.

Another episode in life – ended.

Hindsight Insight

Learning about personalities was one of my top three personal development concepts I learned. They explained the traits for each personality, their strengths and weaknesses, how they would dress, which cars they are likely to drive, how the make decisions, clothes they wear and much more.

In learning about myself I was amazed that I could finally be categorized so easily. Instead of having to fit into a square hole I discovered it was okay to be in a round hole. The Alexander method of using birds to describe personalities is the easiest to understand: The Dove, Owl, Peacock and Eagle. Each of these birds has different traits and these relate to our personality traits. The Dove is caring and works in roles that help people, the Owl is analytical and works in strategic roles, the Peacock is showy and works in creative and people roles, the Eagle is a visionary and works in leadership roles.

Imagine the traits of those four birds. Relate them to yourself and start to get an understanding of yourself and then other people.

_____

_____

_____

_____

_____

_____

Letting go of the past allows you to move forward uncluttered. It is like cleaning out your old clothes or unused furniture. It makes you move forward in life, lighter and without out of date baggage included in your life. Albeit, depending on the circumstance it sometimes is easier said than done. In my book Successful Single Parenting, I talk about the 'leaving' partner and the 'staying' partner. I was the leaver from my marriage; I made the decision to move forward in life so I was scared but enthusiastic and positive, versus the other person who has to live with the consequences. Letting go of an old job to a promotion is easier. Letting go of a belief or changing a direction or stepping out in faith is often with one foot still in the old and one foot tippy toeing in the new world. One step is better than no steps.

Decide where you are on your journey of letting go of the past to embrace the future. What changes to you need to make?

_____

_____

_____

_____

_____

_____

Chapter 14

Life in our Haunted House

Experience is determined by yourself,
not the circumstances in your life.

—Gita Bellini

Over the years, I had a variety of tenants in my studio. I was always a cautious as they were living on my property and had access to the laundry inside. After my first incident, I only allowed it to be used when I was home. However, they usually had friends visit and as the girls were sometimes on their own, I wanted people so they felt safe as well.

One of them had come along with her mother and looked neat and tidy in her work clothes at her interview. When she arrived to move in a few days later, she had on very different clothes a T-shirt with no sleeves and had number of tattoos on her arm. She didn't look like the nice young girl I had interviewed. At the interview she had also asked if she could bring along her four kittens as a car had just killed the mother cat. She assured me it would only be for a week as that had homes for them.

On the first weekend, she disappeared leaving the four kittens in the studio. On Sunday morning the girls heard them meowing from their bedrooms. I called both the tenant and the mother asking them to come and check on the kittens. After numerous telephone calls and a few hours with no replies, I went into the studio and found four kittens locked in the shower. She had left Kentucky fried chicken and potato salad for their food which was now scattered all over the floor.

My girls had two friends to stay for the weekend and as I took out the dirty hungry kittens I had four girls with open arms ready to take them. Each kitten was bathed and then using my hair dryer, warmed and dried back to normal, clean kittens. It was a lovely sight to see and one of those real moment's in life, that lodges in your memory box for the rest of you life, all four girls loving their individual kittens. I didn't have any kitten food but they lapped up the milk and runny scrambled eggs I made them. I don't know who was the happiest to be rescued, the kittens or the four girls who each fell in love with their kitten.

After this episode, the tenant decided to leave. We kept one of the kittens and who was named Mineme. With no mother cat role model it learned to meow sounding just like a bird.

The next Sunday morning, Kirsty knocked on the wall between our rooms, asking me to come into her bed. Carefully I snuck out from my bed as Leila had come in during the night and was still asleep. I climbed the stairs to the Kirsty's bed on the mezzanine floor to see our new kitten snuggled up next to her. Supposedly Mineme had clambered in the window during the night. Next minute the wall was knocked on from my bedroom. Leila had woken and wanted to join us. She arrived and we all were squeezed into Kirsty's bed to cuddle our new kitten. I am not sure who was enjoying it the most. The girls, the kitten or me. Another real moment to treasure.

Life moved on and Mineme became the fourth cat in our lives and another loved member of the family. She was a clever cat and one day I caught her jumping onto my fax/telephone machine that was on a cabinet next to the front door. She walked across it and had her paw on the front door handle as if she was trying to open it. That explained why that machine was always going haywire, but there were other unexplained incidents.

Over time, more interesting events began in the house again. I had moved my office into the room where Leila had initially slept and the nighttime voices had been. I was having trouble with everything electrical in the room. Nothing seemed to work for very long before it malfunctioned. I would repair it and again it would break down. Then one day I was in my bedroom and the hairdryer turned itself on.

Neither of the back bedrooms had very much light. I repainted them both to sunshine yellow color in an attempt to warm them up as one room had turned icy cold. These rooms didn't get any sun so I had a dehumidifier regularly drying the room. This was where I had the initial person rolling over me earlier and Leila had a few strange things happening to her in this room as well. Other little thing's were happening that were unusual. I tried another clearing on the house but to no avail, they continued

During this time, the girls had, unknown to me, started getting more interested in the spirit world. Whereas I kept solution seeking for the challenges that frequented my life I later learned that it is quite normal for young teenage girls to become more interested and start investigating the spirit realms. They had got a library book, and decided to make spirit board with some of their friends and have a séance.

Later I learned that during this process they had contacted the spirit world after one such event and the glass had moved. Another episode and a bad evil spirit transcended which is how I describe it. Prior to this I had learned that the spirits in the house merely needed to move from the physical world to the spiritual world. As the owner of the house they wouldn't hurt me or the girls, but were protecting and playing with us. However, the girls' involvement was something different.

Apparently, these spirits in this realm have a different goal and want to cause harm. Over the winter months, Leila had become disheartened, lethargic and indifferent to life. As much as I thought I was a good parent, I encountered reluctance to her usual activities. Again, I investigated and learned that this is a 'stage of life' as they move through their teen years. However, I wasn't prepared for the next episode.

When I had left my marriage and became a single parent it was also to give the girls a choice about living a positive life or a negative life. I had continued to learn and pass on my personal development information to the girls in a way that I felt helped them learn and understand some of life's challenges and opportunities. I thought I was a good parent, doing a pretty good job, so it was a huge shock when I discovered that Leila had attempted to commit suicide in that bedroom. I was devastated but thankful she had survived.

She had become depressed and I was continually trying to urge her into action. On her first attempt I instantly started searching for new solutions. I found lots of answers and reasons and after some counseling, natural remedies, anti-depressant and vitamins I felt I had found the solutions. I found a friend's daughter who had experienced similar challenges so she had another person to discuss her problems with. Together we organized systems so she had some solutions.

Unfortunately, she tried twice more, each time something different. Every time I was devastated as I tried to help her through her challenges. Each time I searched for more solutions. I was not prepared to lose her! I thought I was guiding her to be positive in her life in an attempt to override the negative thoughts that had been crammed into her head from other sources. Whereas I kept boosting her to try new things, her self-esteem had crashed and she wasn't happy with her life. I only had input when she lived with me and I strived to make that positive.

Her room continued to be cold and she found comfort in her bed. Scared and distraught I kept looking for more answers. After one of her visits to the hospital we were driving along a road that had a cliff face on our way home and I got another clue.

She told me she didn't want to return to her sleep in her bedroom, which surprised me. As soon as she said that, a large stone hit the passenger window where she was sitting. If the window had been opened, she would have gotten hit. We both got a shock and the combination of not wanting to return to her room and the stone I felt something else was happening that needed another solution.

I found a man who works with releasing energy, and he came to perform a clearing on the house and section. He told me once a house is cleared and it becomes a safe haven and new spirits continue to visit. This was what was happening in my house. He said this site had earlier been an area where the spirits left from (whatever that meant), which was why the house was haunted and more spirits returned. He also did some dowsing on the section and found an underground stream in the back yard.

He checked Leila's room, which was the same room I had encountered my first experience, as she was experiencing sleeping challenges again. As soon as he entered the room he said there was a bad spirit in there. He asked for a few minutes alone in there and closed the door. When he emerged he said he had moved it on and the room was clear. As soon as I entered the room, the temperature felt warm, the first time in months. I was amazed. This was our only bad spirit experience in the house.

Apparently, as the girls had played with spirit boards and séances, an extremely bad spirit had entered the room in search of a victim. They look for a vulnerable person who they can influence. Leila was that person. Thus, as well as her susceptibility to the good and positive spirit world, she was also affected to the bad negative spirit world.

He continued checking the room and discovered the electrical cable underneath the floor was beneath Leila's bed that was also affecting her sleeping. Because the room had been so cold she had slept with the electric blanket turned on low. The combination of the mattress and electricity from the blanket and cables under the house was affecting her body's energy field. As soon as he left, I turned her bed around and replaced her innerspring mattress with a rubber one. With the clearing and all the changes in her room she started to sleep well again.

As I guided her to want to live and be happy I worked on her interests. She wanted to ride a horse so I took her to horse riding. I gradually built up the repertoire of things she enjoyed and dangled them in front of her, so she always had something good to look forward to.

As the girls grew into teenagers, the continuous group of visitors started to include boys as well. To enable me to keep track of who was visiting, I made a rule they had to say hello to me before they were allowed to wander into my home to visit the toilet.

I also had many of my friends and family visit the house and again it was a wonderful warm fun house to live in. A new man had entered my life. Initially I didn't tell him about our interesting house. In spite of this, he had a sixth sense and felt something was unusual about it every time he arrived at the end of the drive. Of course I told him it was me, but he assured me there was something else.

After another six months, events were occurring again. This was becoming a hassle, as I spent time searching for solutions. It was taking my time and energy to continuously solve these. As the initial owner has told me, they would not hurt me, but just having fun. Fun for them I thought but a constant challenge for me. I had enough already in my life!

Eventually, I decided it was time for another proper clearing. This time I decided to go back to his house, rather than an in-house visit. It was a cheaper option. As I approached his house, I became very disorientated. I drove up and down streets where I thought he lived and every time felt a push to go somewhere else. After fifteen minutes I eventually knocked on the door of the house which I was sure was his. By this stage I was late and almost in tears and frantic. It was weird. I had never felt this way before. I explained to him what was happening or had happened. He told me spirit does this to people because they don't want to get moved on. I was much relieved it was normal and I was okay. These spirit encounters were becoming a bit of a problem in my life. I was busy enough without these experiences.

When we stared the clearing, it confirmed there were a few spirits again. Apparently, because I was living in the house and receptive to them (not that I realized I was). They just came rolling on in. One of the spirits was a seventeen-year-old boy who had drowned, and the other was a very interesting situation. It was someone who my partner knew from over fifteen years ago who hadn't passed over, as they call it. Neither of these people wanted to go or move over for their individual reasons. My energy man helped them to realize their dilemma, stuck between two worlds and completed their transition. I did not really understand this process, all I was concerned with was the girls and I were safe and life would revert to normality, whatever that was. It was a great relief when the situation was complete.

I wasn't fully understanding the 'behind the scenes' of all these situations. I did not have the interest or time to do research. In essence I trusted the process and what felt right. All I was interested in was that we were all okay. In hindsight I was being educated about the spirit world in some of its different forms.

So, once again I was left with a cleared and normal house.

Hindsight Insight

Life is a gazillion moments. Albeit, there are some that we remember easily, like when the man walked on the moon, or when I heard Elvis or John Lennon passed away or when you achieved something. However, between these moments are other real moments that truly make us love life. These are with people we love, places and experiences that we treasure. Our task in life is to create as many of these as possible as well as take notice when these are happening in our life. It could mean, saying 'no' to a task to enable you to say 'yes' to a real moment.

Are you taking note of your real moments in life? What do you need to include more of in your life?

_____

_____

_____

_____

_____

_____

When searching for answers it is important to keep open minded to new ideas. If you had found a solution with your present thinking, you would not need to continue looking for answers. Within every idea, is the possibility of the solution as you expand your thinking to embrace something new. One of the keys is to ensure it will result in a positive outcome versus a negative outcome as you keep seeking until you feel satisfied with your answer. Sometimes these may come from your past when you have had read an article or had a conversation and the problem you are experiencing is pushing you to pursue that concept further for your solution.

What answers have you sought in the past and are still seeking? Do you need to expand your thoughts, values and beliefs to accept them?

_____

_____

_____

_____

_____

_____

Chapter 15

The Message

Reach high for stars lie hidden in your soul,
Dream deep, for every dream precedes the goal.

—Pamela Vaull Starr

With New Zealand being the first country in the World Time Zone we greeted the new millennium first. I celebrated the arrival at a concert in the Auckland domain. It had been a warm drizzly evening with thousands of people gathered to welcome the new century. Globally, the whole world was greeting the new millennium. Millions of the worlds' population were anticipating new beginnings, changes ahead and awakening to new and interesting ideas. Other skeptics predicted doom and gloom. It was also a time of change for me.

Juggling my busy life as a single working parent for fifteen years and the accompanied challenges had me continuously stressed. I was in burnout mode and exhausted and every holidays I got sick. I knew I couldn't continue life in the fast lane, and mine definitely wasn't the normal sex, drugs and rock and roll. I remember thinking years earlier before I had left my marriage, that had I stayed I would have had serious health problems, or be six feet under the ground. So, although it wasn't with partying and fun that had exhausted me, as a single parent, there is no-one to help or look after you, with a cup of tea, word of comfort, help out with jobs, hug or discuss your challenges when you needed it. I needed to learn how to juggle, improve life and look after myself. It meant I needed to include 'time-outs' into my life instead of working at a zillion miles a day.

As I had learned the Playcentre philosophy, 'learning through play,' I had always included the girls in everything I was doing around the house. They had learned to cook, clean and help out with household and jobs out in the garden. All these skills would help mould their future and it was great when they would cook dinner and I could chill out. Often the chores didn't get finished or completed to my standard, but I learned that as long as the vacuuming was done, or the dishes done before bed, it was okay. There was no need to sweat the small stuff, I was in survival mode and sometimes mediocre was okay and there is more than one way for everything in life.

In the past, when the girls were away, I had relaxed or gone sailing every other weekend. On the boat it was great; I couldn't do any housework or even walk further from bow to stern and was forced to sit still and relax, one with nature as I sat out amongst the wind, waves and night time stars. When they stopped visiting their father, this changed and as mothers know, we have to constantly adapt to the changes in our children's lives. We do when they are born into our life, when they crawl, walk, talk and go to school and here was another change.

I had finished work as a full-time tutor and was working part-time and developing my coaching business and had a tenant in my studio and my rental property.

Trying to be healthy was a constant challenge. I was allowing myself some time out to regenerate myself and regain a healthier perspective and direction in my life. Every year it was always on my goals list to improve on my health. Regularly I went for a morning walk in an effort to get fit. I walked down to the bottom of the street, through a walkway and around a couple of the local streets. It was an enjoyable walk, twenty to thirty minutes long, depending which streets I meandered along. The tree-lined street with a hill was my favorite. I could walk up one side and down the other side and glimpse a city view. It was a tidy street with pleasant houses and lovely gardens. It was a busy street as the children walked to the nearby school and people drove off to work.

It was early in the year 2000, a new era, a new millennium. The day had started normally with the girls getting organized to catch the bus to school. I had walked my usual route; I was deep in thought about the tasks for the day and the future ahead. I was through the walkway and a few meters into my favorite street.

Then it happened!

I stopped in my tracks. A very deep almost husky voice boomed loud around me. It was like a stereo on full blast with the bass on!

I looked around the street. It was empty. I expected to see someone with a loudspeaker on the top of their car, like we see during the elections. But, the street was deserted. It was eight o'clock in the morning. There should have been activity in the street. But there was no children walking to school, no dogs, no cats and no cars on the road. Everything was perfectly still. I wondered, "who is talking to me?"

The voice said:

"Start a self-esteem day."

Then, a tangled, clear, garbled message zapped into my mind . . . It was a blueprint of ideas that scrambled into my thoughts . . .

I saw a vision of a screen. A white line scrolled along the bottom with words on it The person on the screen looked like one of our most famous rugby players. He was on the right side of the screen with a ball in his hand running with a grandstand of people in the background.

In the next vision of a screen they were talking about a negative experience of their life. Then they finishing saying "but I chose to take a positive action to become successful"

It continued for about thirty seconds. I had never seen anything similar. In the year 2000 in New Zealand we did not have the scrolls along the bottom of the TV screen like we do on television today.

I got the impression that the person could have done something that was negative but choose a positive road in life instead.

Mystified, I looked behind me but there was still no one in sight. I

asked myself:

- Who spoke to me?
- What had happened?
- Where did that come from?

From my past experiences of receiving ideas to 'write my life story' I had an answer – but it seemed bizarre!

- Who was giving these to me?

- Was it from the universe or GOD?

- Or if not God, then who? They were asking me to help others.

- WHY ME?

It didn't make sense to me and I thought I've really, really 'LOST' it this time! Who do I think I am, to do that? I can't do that! I am not good enough!

I can't recall if I continued walking or went home in shocked surprise. I rang a friend and told her my story. She was as perplexed as I was and I can't recall what she said. Now ten years later and knowing her as I do, she might have said, "Well, you've been given a job to do. Get on with it."

I was open to new ideas, but I had two teenage children, work and income to earn and lots of other things to do.

. . . So I shelved The MESSAGE I'd received! It frequently crossed my mind:

Did God Speak to ME and give me a job to do?

At that stage, I didn't have the courage to tell anyone else or do anything about it.

It wasn't until after four years of additional personal development and learning, attending Unity in Auckland, talking to the minister and reading the Daily Word that my thoughts changed to *Who do I think I am not doing this work?*

My thoughts had changed, therefore my action would change. I now had more courage, insights and knowledge. Once again I had to move right out of my comfort, further than I have or could ever imagine I was capable of and put myself right on the cutting edge of life. Other winners and successful people had done it. So could I!

In my rational mind I knew I would never think of an idea of this magnitude. Nothing similar had ever crossed my mind, so this idea was far greater than my mind comprehended. Additionally, it was for the good of the world and ultimately good for me as I was extending my comfort zone. I would be forced to learn and grow and I assumed only good could arise from it.

Later in life, I read a book about soul writing where you sat and wrote until you had nothing else to write. You would choose a topic you needed to resolve. In essence, you would write until you started to write automatically. At this stage, you would begin writing words of great wisdom, words that provided you the answers you needed that would propel you forward in your life. This was called 'soul writing' and the reason that one would know it was spirit or soul messaging, was because all the answers provided were messages of unconditional love for oneself and the world.

In retrospect, I thought this about my message. It was a message of unconditional love that would propel me out of my comfort zone onto an exciting journey in life. No harm could come to me or anyone else. It was an unconditional message of love for mankind and I needed to rise to the challenge.

And, it was one line of words made famous by Nelson Mandela that was the catalyst to my new thinking. Marianne Williamson wrote the poem in the Course of Miracles.

Our Deepest Fear

Our deepest fear is not that we are inadequate,

Our deepest fear is that we are powerful beyond measure.

It is our light, not our darkness that most frightens us.

We ask ourselves, who am I to be

brilliant, gorgeous, talented fabulous?

Actually, who are you not to be?

You are a child of God.

Your playing small does not serve the world.

There is nothing enlightened about shrinking so that other people won't feel insecure around you.

We were born to make manifest the glory of God that is within us.

It is not just in some of us, it is in everyone.

And as we let our own light shine,

we unconsciously give other people permission to do the same.

As we are liberated from our own fear,

our presence automatically, liberates others.

Thus my *'playing small does not serve the world,'* in fact it didn't serve me either. God had given me a message . . . and according to all the numerology and soul journey information I had learned, this was my journey! As I learned and shared I let my light shine. I overcame my fear and helped others. Now it made sense and like an extended version of the Nike quote, "I just had to do it!"

I decided I either had to 'shape up' to my life mission or 'ship out' of life and forever be a failure not taking up the biggest and scariest challenge that would move me right out of my comfort zone forever. The world had greeted this new millennium with anticipated change, I had as well, so it was time to let go of old thinking which is easier said than done, and open my mind to new ideas, thoughts and a new way of thinking. I decided to shape up!

Hindsight Insight

There is a saying about our mind is like a parachute. Once it is exposed and opened to a new idea it will never regain the same size, like a rubber band once it is stretched, it will never again be exactly the same size. This is the same as our thoughts. Ideas are constantly bombarding our mind. It could be an advertisement or an 'aha!' moment, when you realize that was the answer to you were seeking for a particular challenge you are experiencing. Some ideas you act upon, others you dismiss. Generally, the ones that move us forward and are within our comfort zone are the easiest for us to act upon. Those that are outside our comfort zone, we are challenged by. These ideas are our critical turning points in life, that steer us on our upward journey.

What ideas or 'aha' moments do you need to rethink? If they are propelling you forward in life, find the courage to act upon them.

'Shoulder-tapping' is a phrase I use and occurs in our life sometimes without us being aware of it. It could be suggested you apply for a job, visit a place or many other reasons. Synchronicity and co-incidences occur in our life without us being aware we are being directed. After my years of learning and the reason for these hindsight insights is that we are supported, pushed and prodded from both the physical and spiritual world. It can come in the form of a message from a clairvoyant or anyone else that focuses on something positive that propels you forward. It can be your gut-reaction or intuition that leads you to do something, visit somewhere or call or talk to somebody.

What situations have you been 'shoulder-tapped' about or had a sense you should do? Are they guiding you to learn and steer you towards your life purpose? Have you ignored them and do you need to rethink and act upon them?

_____

_____

_____

_____

_____

_____

Chapter 16

Americas' Cup

When the going gets tough, that's when the
'tough get going.'

—Joseph P. Kennedy

Being bitter and twisted about the hard times I've experienced in life has always been a waste of energy. I had to forgive myself for any past decisions and not hold anger towards myself or anyone else. I've had lessons to learn, as everyone in life and everyone has different situations and circumstances. I made the choices, learned from them and am who I am today because of them. Another valuable lesson was embracing the concept that whatever decision I made at any point of time, was the best I was capable of making then. Five seconds, minutes or years later I may have made a different decision.

As a single mum with two dependent children my responsibility was to ensure the well-being of my family. As the sole income earner and with minimum additional financial support it made my dreams seem more distant and unattainable. It was challenging, along with continued challenges from my ex-partner. It drained me physically, mentally, financially and spiritually.

In hindsight, when I left my marriage I never thought I would be alone for ten or fifteen years. I thought I would meet up with a new partner much earlier, but this didn't happen and I was okay with that. Instead, I was determined to achieve my goal of 'getting our lives' on track and the girls were top priority. I wanted to achieve the goals I set myself when I walked out of my marriage. I needed to be a positive role model and guide the girls to become self-supporting members of society.

One 'aha' moment was when I realized I didn't have to own everything myself. I was independent but I could sail on someone else's boat, live in someone else's house and although I was the breadwinner in the family, it was okay if I didn't achieve all this on my own. Over the years of 'going it alone' I had forgotten about the philosophy of sharing with a partner which although was part of my plan, was not top priority.

My dreams were important and my salvation and striving for them became part of my purpose.

Backtracking to 1995 and New Zealand, things were at a virtual standstill. Patriotic kiwis wore red socks the day Team New Zealand won the world-renowned famous yacht race, the America's Cup. The regatta was held in San Diego, America. Most eyes were glued to television sets but not the group of Kiwi SWAP adventurers I was with. We were tramping around Lake Waikaremoana, a lake known for its isolation and beauty in the middle of the North Island of the New Zealand.

We all wore our red socks, which was a symbol of patriotism to our New Zealand yachting challenge. We realized it would be impossible for us to watch a television and see the race in the tramper's huts on the mountain.

Besides when we departed from the low-lying valley in the Urewera National park our mobile phones did not receive any reception. Consequently we didn't expect to hear the results of the final race for the challenge for a few days. As a sailor, that was a tragedy!

For a novice hiker, having a heavy pack strapped to my back was a challenge. I couldn't stand up straight otherwise I felt like I would topple backwards. I had to concentrate staying balanced and on the simple task of placing one foot in front of the other. After a few hours and climbing steadily up a steep mountain, the silence was shattered when a group of Japanese hikers quickly approached us coming down the track. "We've won, we've won!" they chanted as they danced down towards us. Their packs were obviously empty, but someone's mobile phone had worked higher up the mountain and they'd managed to hear the good news about the yacht race.

Team New Zealand's 'Black Magic,' the financial underdogs, but not small fry in spirit and expertise had managed to triumph over all odds. They had conquered the world's most sought-after yachting trophy, the famous America's Cup, from the Americans.

Hugs were exchanged in celebration. It was impossible to have a drink to celebrate in good Kiwi fashion at the time. Our alcohol was stored in plastic milk bottles somewhere in the heavy packs. We voted celebrations would take place in the hiker's hut on the mountain peak for the evening's entertainment.

The tramping continued and dodging the tree roots on the path became an increasing challenge for me. However, it was still possible to soak in the magic of their surroundings as the sunshine filtered through the native bush. During my passionate exchange with my eyes glued to the ground, a dream emerged. I was going to be involved with the America's Cup Challenge, when it came to New Zealand. My creative and lateral thinking brainstormed for ideas of products for the marketplace. I created a musical CD with sailing music. Finally the possibility of losing the family house and the financial loss if the product didn't sell was too great a risk, so that idea was discarded.

Intuition is a great skill that we women have and the idea of a telephone call and asking to be involved had positive results.

Sir Peter Blake, the skipper and leader who had led his team of sailors to win, said:

> You can make any dream real if you work away at it long enough.

Consequently, I was also not one to give up on a dream. My background included travel and tourism so when I first met with the organizers I was asked to be a tour guide for tourists who wished to see the Cup.

A flinch of my face answered that question. Alternatively I could be out on the water helping in the boats. Passionate about the sea and sailing and with my first book titled, *Sailing – a Different Course,* and being a boatie for over twenty-five years, of course the answer was astoundingly - YES!

Juggling my family and work life made it possible for me to be out on the water. Attending my first meeting was interesting as I walked into a room of males. I thought I was in the wrong place and with no friendly faces I had the distinct feeling of entering into man's territory. It was like one of those tourist tee shirts, covered in white sheep with one black sheep. I was the black one and I sheepishly strolled towards the back rows.

However, determination and a dream to follow meant I returned to the second meeting. I was still the black sheep but thankfully, a friendly grandfather took me under his wing. Later he told me I reminded him of his daughter.

Creating dreams has previously dropped me in unexpected places.

A few years earlier I was scheduled to be in a small rubber dinghy on patrol, to keep the racecourse free for the finish of the Whitbread round the world yacht race. It was a cold rainy day and I would have been soaked! However, a late change of plans and I was whisked aboard to crew on the fifty foot launch with the international media photographers aboard. The launch cruised inside the coastguard and police security boats to ensure good photos for the media. As I looked down from the bridge of the launch, I thanked my lucky stars I had scored a change of boat. I was aboard the closest boat allowed to the incoming round the world fleet. There were hundreds of spectator boats on the water and it was chaos out in the mainstream and would have been bedlam in the waves in our little rubber dinghy among the crowd of boats.

For a person passionate about sailing it was awesome. The same happened with the America's Cup regatta.

The role of the patrol boats for the America's Cup Challenge was to ensure the correct setting up of the course and also keep any of the spectator boats off the racing course. Boats were positioned at either end of the windward course and angled out port and starboard with their buoys in place and then allocated an area to patrol between nearby buoys. This meant there is a huge area of water allocated for the America's Cup course.

If there was a wind shift all the buoys had to be hauled in and repositioned again. Three people were on board each boat a skipper, radio person and someone to manhandle the buoys.

Anywhere on the course would have great for me. It's a spectacular view watching the yachts spin on their keel, maneuver effortlessly and hear the sound of the winches grinding and sails setting. Then there's the awesome sight of the huge spinnakers puffed full with wind as the yachts beat down the course towards you.

In living my dream, the universe again dropped me into a great spot on the course.

The start and finish box is where the yachts must enter within five minutes prior to the start of the race. Outmanoeuvring the competitor ensures the best start for each yacht. At close quarters the yachts are even more magnificent as they steer towards the outskirts of the imaginary boxed area, spin on their keel and then speed off in another direction. It's the best place on the course to see the yachts in action. That's where I was. The universe dropped me in greater places than I imagine myself. This quote sums up my journey and sense of achievement:

If it weren't difficult it wouldn't be worthwhile doing.

—Sir Peter Blake

And it *was* difficult to juggle life in pursuit of a dream. I was positioned there for the start and finish of every race in the regatta and once again in the closest patrol boats.

Fun is an integral part of my personality and daily I managed to slip something on board. A water pistol, cheer leader pom poms to shake when we won a race and of course some whistles and other items for our final celebration.

So, my dream from 1995 from when I had plodded around Lake Waikaremoana had me involved in the defence of the America's Cup with Sir Peter Blake and Team New Zealand for the five nil win over the Italian boat, Prada. New Zealand went wild! It was great supporting two things I loved, my sport and my country.

Discussing my next dream with the organizer, I told him I'd like to helm (steer) an America's Cup yacht. He told me it was impossible. "Never," was my reply. "It will happen." Somehow, and it did!

There was no indication that any previous America Cup yachts were coming to sail on Auckland's harbour. While attending a conference a few years later, my daughter called a radio station during a competition and was allocated a seat aboard NZL40 (a past America's Cup Yacht) for me. So, my motto is now: Dream it and make it a reality.

'Sink or swim' is always a choice. Swim has always been my answer and life's challenges always ensured I overcame the adversities. In the pursuit of my dream I'd focused and was determined to succeed. I've always thought: if other people can do it, so can I.

Moving with the times meant other changes were about to happen. As I downsized my home and moved to Waterview another journey began.

After I discovered Leila was wagging and not committing to her schoolwork I realized another solution was needed. I decided I shouldn't be paying for her to attend school and instead she could work and pay me rent. Consequently, I allowed her to leave school, which was a hard decision to make. This didn't align with my goal for her education and she was not moving ahead at high school.

She was a people person and loved animals and had a special affiliation with them. In her schoolwork experience she had worked at the zoo and she had loved her part time job at Bird Barn working with the animals. As a result we investigated her studying at Unitec Technical Institute to start a vet nursing course. She was too young so instead worked in an office for a year. She hated working on a computer all day, which I knew she would. Still, she decided she didn't want to sit on a computer for the rest of her life. At the end of twelve months she was old enough and accepted for a vet nurse course and was committed to succeeding.

She had moved out and lived in an apartment while working, and after a few miss-haps and learning experiences arrived back home to move into the two-bedroom unit with me and decided to return to study. Hurriedly I had to turn the garage into another room for her.

I was thrilled at her enthusiasm at new topics and willingness to learn about animals. This was her passion and I was pleased when her weekends were now spent studying accounting, biology and topics which she had dismissed at school as boring and useless. Now she was on track in her life using her natural gifts and talents. At the end of year one she passed every topic first time and her confidence soared. She had part time jobs with vet clinics while she studied and loved that work.

At school her dream had been to work in a wildlife park. It had seemed impossible to her but now she could see it could become a reality. I was a proud mum when she received her certificates and I think she was proud of herself. Her confidence and esteem had soured again. Leila decided to continue into her second year of study with the same passion and enthusiasm as her first year.

Suddenly Kirsty wanted to move back home and closer to Unitec for her last year of study. She wasted an hour a day traveling and we lived only ten minutes from Unitec. Still the artist, she had chosen to go into design and get a Bachelors of Design. She had always been a committed student and achieved great results. Hers was a four-year course and she spent hours creating fantastic intricate models and designs for her course. They were fantastic and consequently she landed a dream job, designing bars.

When Kirsty had left we lived in a five bedroom house, now I lived in a two bedroom apartment where I thought I would be living on my own. When Leila had moved back into an outside bedroom and me working from home and redecorating the unit along with Kerry visiting, the unit was full and life became chaotic.

Kerry had purchased a new cliff-top house at the beach a year earlier and which we visited every weekend. Our work was in the city and it had saved him hours of traveling living there. His big contract was ending and we decided to move to the beach and let Kirsty and Leila live in my unit.

It was a great decision for their studies but lousy decisions for my bank balance, they were the worst and untidiest tenants I'd ever had, studying and working rather than doing house-work. However, in the end they were both qualified in their selected fields, which was a more important achievement.

My goal when I had left my marriage with the girls was to direct them into their passions and uniqueness rather than clone them into who I would like them to be. An important lesson for parents!

I was proud when my nineteen-year goal was achieved and Mum and I attended Leila's graduation in the morning and Kirsty's graduation in the afternoon, both on the same day. I was pleased they had overcome all the challenges from their past, and moved away from some of their friends and both girls had dreams with positive outlooks on life.

Hindsight Insight

Our soul urges us forward and we all have different urges and subsequent challenges. The theory we have past lives is supported when family members have unrelated interests, abilities and goals. This reinforces the idea that we are alive on earth to fulfill our soul's journey with one another.

What dreams from your soul are unfulfilled? What changes do you need to get on track in your life?

_____

_____

_____

_____

_____

_____

An era can cover any period in our life. It could be a job, relation-ship, possession, lifestyle or country. As challenging or as easy as it may be, we need to bless it for the opportunity it gave us to learn about life and ourselves. My marriage was one of the best and worst times of my life. It had two wonderful outcomes, my children. I was angry with myself for being a softie, getting married and becoming a single parent. None of those were on my to-do list and I had to forgive myself to move forward. However the benefits were my era jolted me back onto a path of self-discovery, which was wonderful.

What eras do you have in your life that you need to adjust your thinking about? What do you need to forgive yourself for?

_____

_____

_____

_____

_____

_____

Chapter 17

In the Pursuit of Happyness

*Each person on Earth is like a seed, a dormant shell of pure
potential, waiting to be transformed into a flower. We may not
have discovered some of our divine attributes, but they are safely
tucked within us, waiting to be called forth. Our perfect potential
– the very essence of our wholeness – is there inside.*

—Daily Word

In shaping up to 'my potential' I was getting a sense that I was always dangled a carrot in the form of 'a message' in front of me. When all else seemed 'out of order' in my life, the insights from the messages I had received spurred me forward on a defined path. Consequently, I was always learning and trying something new, therefore always out of my comfort zone.

From my years from when I was bullied at high school at fifteen or sixteen, I was feeling unhappy on the inside. It wasn't a nice feeling and it felt something was wrong in my life. It wasn't until I took control of my life when I walked out of my marriage with my two daughters when I was thirty-three years old that I felt freedom again; when I took charge of my life.

It was now 2003, and with the messages I had received I started scheming how I could achieve them . . . I had a sense of purpose. If I could earn enough money, I could start creating these ideas. In hindsight this was still not in the right order. I hadn't brought these messages to the forefront of my life. They were simmering, but not boiling. But at least I started the journey.

While I was a travel tutor I had joined the National Speakers Association in Auckland and mixed and mingled with people who motivated and trained others. It felt the right place for me to be and for years I attended as a bystander, learning but not ready to implement. While I had full responsibility of the girls, I needed to be bringing in a regular income, rather than follow the path of self-employment. It was time for change and gradually, I gathered courage and fine-tuned some of my stories and skills into presentations. I attended the conferences held in New Zealand and when I was the Auckland President, attended the Australian National Speakers Association conference in 2006.

Money was still tight (it was great to learn this is a personality trait and can be conquered) and luckily as happens, the universe went to work and Kerry and I were staying in a friend's apartment in Broadbeach in Surfers Paradise. It was payback for when they had stayed with us for a week. It was the front apartment and we looked out over the park and palm trees onto the beautiful Surfers Paradise beach. We had a swimming pool, spa and underground parking for the week, which was useful for our bike adventure.

The day before the conference Kerry rented a Harley motorbike and I had my first Harley ride. I achieved another of my dreams. He drove us down to Byron's Beach on a Harley Centennial fat boy motorcycle, with me calling out, "We're doing it, we're doing it." When we arrived down there he asked me what was going on . . . , I told him about declaring one of my dreams coming true as I lived it. Obviously once again he thought I was a little bit mad!

It was an hour's drive and we had learned the 'Harley nod' to other bikes on the ride there. It wasn't until later that I found Kerry was petrified because the bike was so big and heavy and swayed with the wind. We learned later that it was because it had no spokes in the wheels, whereas when they have spokes the wind travels through the wheels rather than pushing against them. After lunch and a wander we decided to drive back a different route via Tweed Heads. We stopped for a coffee and literally slid off the bike, hardly able to stand up and walk. We must have been a comical sight as we waddled into the coffee shop; two fifty-year-olds trying to be teenagers again. We had the Harley for twenty-four hours and planned to take it out after dinner and see the sights of Surfers through new eyes, from the back of a motorbike. The best of plans often don't work. We were so tired we fell asleep at nine o'clock.

The next morning, stiff and revived, I was driven to the conference at a five star hotel on the Harley. We caught the eyes of the security guys, who initially must have thought we were a threat as they kept watching us. I'm sure they changed their mind when they saw how in-elegantly I slid of the bike. However, Kerry decided to give them a bit of a thrill, and revved the bike up, which sounded deep and throaty as only a Harley can, as he whizzed away. He had a couple of hours before he had to deliver it back and took it for a spin, trying out his skills from his youth when he owned a bike.

At my first Australian conference in Surfers I had an opportunity to speak about the International Self-Esteem Day, which I had started to promote. I was putting myself out on a limb with this and had people who were interested in sharing the concept.

Because I had been busy before leaving New Zealand I needed to work on my presentation in Surfers Paradise. I was sent the usual challenges to overcome. First, my computer appeared to crash and I thought I had lost my presentation. Then I received a phone call from my brother in New Zealand. I was in turmoil because I thought the only reason he would ring was because something had happened to Dad who was in hospital with a stroke.

Over the years of personal growth I had learned hundreds of lessons and tips about life. Some I had implemented and remembered, some I wasn't ready for or maybe felt they didn't apply to me. One important tip was how to react in a crisis.

Instead of wondering whether something had happened to dad, I had to change my thoughts to, "I can't do anything about it right now, and I don't know the answer." Then I could concentrate on my presentation and I went with that gut feeling. When I checked later, my brother had just pushed my number by mistake, so thankfully I hadn't got in a panic.

I had another hiccup when I had to give my presentation along with two others in a room with forty or fifty people. I had been asked to speak by the organizers on my topic of International Self-Esteem Day. The presenters prior to me gave very different presentations to what I was giving. When I was introduced there was an unusual comment by the emcee which felt like a bit of a put down. It surprised me and quickly I inserted a new sentence to the beginning of my presentation. I assured the audience that the organizer had asked me specifically to speak about this topic although it was different type of international speaking from the previous speakers. The others were speaking about how to get work in Asia and then the United States, whereas I was speaking about an event they could promote to their database and help people.

I had another couple of 'aha' moments. Those moments when your brain comes up with an idea or concept way out of your normal mode of thinking and goes 'click,' this is for me!

The first one was when a lady was taking video shots to use in the Oprah show and I had a flashing thought, I could or should do that! (I'm not sure which).

The second one was when I was attending a seminar. We were asked to write down the first answer that came into your mind (and I had learned in the past, this was your intuition, creative side or universe) giving you the correct answer. The question was what did we think we were worth. The answer that flashed into my mind was twenty million. I shook my head as the amount took me by surprise. Twenty million! How on earth was I going to earn that? I asked myself. And the next question was what would I do with all that money?

After I had the luxuries of house, car, and boat and helped out the family I would have lots left, then I realized it would be used to expand the International Self-Esteem Trust. That was some insightful carrot!

I left the conference with my head buzzing with ideas.

On the plane coming home, the movie playing for the passengers was "The Pursuit of Happyness," which I hadn't seen. I had the window seat and decided to spend my time going through my notes from the conference. Out of the corner of my eye I could see the movie Kerry was watching. I didn't have my earplugs in so couldn't hear any dialogue but kept glancing over.

> *Then it happened, like a rush of 'coming home feeling' and euphoria but not déjà vu, another of those huge experiential 'AHA' moments.*
>
> *I was getting used to these, so just sat quietly through the experience. Everything else goes into the background . . . and the focus of my attention was not on me . . . but on my thoughts and how they were making me feel. Tears started to well up in*

my eyes and roll down my cheeks. So that's it . . . that's how I am supposed to make the twenty million dollars . . . wow!

"The Pursuit of Happyness" was a true story. The message I was getting was that I was to make a movie of my life story. That message I received over fifteen years ago now made more sense to me. When I had received it, I hadn't written a word. Eventually I had thought the message to mean, write about my 'experiences' which when all my books and eBooks added up, did just that. They were about what had happened to me . . . and what I had learned. So – of course I was thinking I was on track.

But now . . . with the 'twenty million' revelation I was stumped – until now. I was to turn my life story into a movie! Like "The Pursuit of Happyness," turn the learning, lessons, journey into a movie . . . and that was where the dollars would eventuate. But along with that . . . my next query was who and how?

My next answer was the best in the world . . . and in fact New Zealand. That was another 'wow' for me . . . as these messages were 'way outside' my comfort zone . . . and my own thoughts. Where were these coming from? I had only one answer! Divine Guidance . . . God!

This time I can't recall a specific voice calling . . . but the words were certainly being processed in my brain . . . and along with my feelings and the sense of euphoria . . . it made sense.

All the messages were making more sense! The best way to spread the word globally about the importance of self-esteem was via the medium that millions of people used; technology. Movies, DVD and the Internet – just like "The Pursuit of Happyness" movie.

I can't recall this part exactly . . . the idea of an interactive movie. I sensed that it came at the same time . . . but my mind was already catapulted into 'space out mode'. And then of course, there is a New Zealand cast . . . and made in New Zealand movie. We were the first country in the world, we were leaders of others; entrepreneurs, and all the ideas about New Zealand being Godzone and although a little country we were respected for our creative ideas and known on the world stage. We tried things; companies came here to test the market, lots of information and back up stuff popped into my mind. Bit by bit, these thoughts and ideas came as well, I can't recall exactly.

I sat in the plane, dumbfounded. Tears rolled down my face. I wasn't sobbing or crying, just tears running down my cheeks. If Kerry had looked over, he would have wondered what was going on. Thankfully he was concentrating on the movie.

After a few minutes or was it five or ten, I can't recall. I seemed to have finished receiving my next mission . . . in fact in hindsight it was a bit like "Mission Impossible," and on the TV they made it possible and this is what I was being guided to do as well.

And so I wiped away my tears in case the hostess saw me and I sat dumbstruck in this latest revelation. As I write this now I think, "Oh My Goodness! WOW! So that is what these haunting messages have been about!"

Hindsight Insight

Our feelings are our inside response to things that happen to us in the outer world. Our responses happen within a nanosecond and it seems hard to believe that there five steps in the process.

We have the event, interpret it, respond, decide how, and then express it either to the outside world or internalize it. A good example is when we are happy we laugh out loud, when we are sad, we cry. Those outward expressions are matching our feelings. Life goes awry when we are sad but show a happy face. You cover up your real feelings and the 'real person.' I was an expert for many years until I saw my miss-take. It is human nature to create good feelings and it is still the same, you just need to get the formula right and align yourself to your greatness.

What feelings are you experiencing that are not being expressed? Do you have any from the past you need to resolve?

_____

_____

_____

_____

_____

_____

The universe is prodding us to stay on track in our life with our inner compass, our intuition or gut feelings. Then we have 'aha' moments or insights that suddenly are like light bulbs in our thoughts. An idea, a realization, a knowing, a word from a friend, song, stranger, or words you read in a book. These are all insights giving us a direction to follow in life. Some people pick up on them early in life, some latter in life like me, some people never. Everyone has free will to choose whether to act on these, but they are guiding lights to every individual becoming their best and finding happiness and success in life. In essence the 'Be, Do, Have' principal.

What insights have you had in your past that you have ignored? If you are searching, how can you start to act upon them?

_____

_____

_____

_____

_____

_____

Chapter 18

Heaven on Earth

Do not follow where the path may lead.
Go instead where there is no path and leave a trail.

—~Ralph Waldo Emerson

When I first saw Kerry, the song "Some Enchanted Evening" from the famous movie "My Fair Lady" was playing. He was dancing with another lady and I thought, "I'd like someone who dances like that!" It wasn't until weeks later that we finally met at another event on the other side of Auckland city I discovered he was the same man. Once we started chatting, it was strange because we discovered we had been living a few streets away from each other for twenty years, and had also gone to the same tennis club over the same times.

He wanted to meet a lady who wanted to run a motel with him so I immediately dismissed any relationship and he looked out for a lady who had that on their goal list. A few weeks later I wanted a partner for a ball. He told me he couldn't dance, but would come as my partner anyway. Once we were there his whacky sense of humor was revealed. He could dance and had been teasing me. I discovered he was the same man I had seen dancing earlier and fate had brought us together. I decided I'd like this man for me, albeit our goals were different.

There is an interesting theory that our souls keep close to one another until they or we are ready to meet and spend time together, to complete our journeys. Thus when we meet a person and immediately feel connected and get along together, like long lost friends, this may prove the theory. It's also answers the falling in love at first sight notion. I have meet girlfriends like this who feel like sisters and twice it has happened to me when meeting a new partner. We have tip toed around each other for a period of time and then we finally meet. Consequently, I now embrace the theory that souls keep close until they meet.

If we believe the concepts 'we are here to learn' and 'our souls spend time together to finish their work,' then ours is an interesting relationship. I have needed all my personal awareness knowledge to survive. Both of us needed to learn different aspects about life and relationships. The universe has dropped me in a house living on a cliff face at the beach, far exceeding my personal expectations. Thus I have been cared for in the physical/financial realm of life. In return the universe has dropped me into my partner's life, to coach about the mental/spiritual side of life.

I believe it is our journey to create our own heaven on earth. We have free will to choose to work at it daily or not. After being single and independent for fifteen years and making all the major decisions, I had to rethink how to compromise and work as a team creating a win/win relationship. Each of us providing our skills, attributes and personalities to be supportive in a team and supported as an individual on our separate life journeys.

The physic of mankind is the male is the hunter and the gather, as Kerry phrases it, and the female, as I phrase it, is the nurturer and homemaker. To a great extend this primeval situation has evolved in our relationship. Once an independent person who had to make every decision, I've learned to let go of some responsibilities. However, as relationships move through the changes in society over the last century and then update ourselves with twenty-first century expectations and role changes, our relationship evolves.

Albeit, Kerry has learned about our spiritual visitors and can some-times sense them himself. At the beach we live close to an old Pa site and have had more interesting experiences.

With the myriad of television programs, movies and books, society is learning more about the spiritual presence in our physical world. As we do, people are becoming less fearful and gradually like me, learning to use this presence as guiding lights in life. In some of the latest movies, this message is being expanded with the phrase from

"Avatar" in *'I see you'* and from the movie "Angels and Demons" with *'Angels guide me.'*

I keep sensing that when I am on track to my life purpose, I experience a series of obstacles to overcome. Throughout my life I have called these tests that are challenges to ensure I am really committed to my life work and journey.

One morning I received a telephone call asking if I would like to be involved in a DVD called "Your Guide to True Happiness."

"Yes!" I said and experienced an overwhelming sense of coming home as I burst into tears. I went to calm myself down and sat on our cliff-face when I had an urgent desire to write a poem, which I hadn't for years. Later, when it came time to filming the DVD, the universe sent me more that its usual challenges.

The first two filming dates I was unable to attend. On the third time I could not find the new address he had moved to. The forth time, I was ready to walk out the door and a huge thunderstorm erupted and hit the area. They called and told me the noise on the roof of the recording studio was so loud, they could not continue working. The fifth and final time was scheduled for a Saturday morning in his studio. My week turned to custard:

- On Saturday night Kerry's father passed away and Sunday and Monday was spent organizing the funeral.

- On Tuesday it was Leila's twenty-first birthday and we had a family dinner.

- On Wednesday, amidst the chaos, I had to shop for an outfit for an awards night, which I was attending on Thursday.

- On Wednesday night Kerry's mother passed away.

- On Thursday morning I had a workshop.

- On Thursday night I had the awards night that Kerry decided he would still attend with me.

- On Friday we had a double funeral.

- On Friday night I had his family returning to our home for dinner.

- On Saturday I had the filming. By this stage I was shattered and living on vitamin tablets and arnica, as well as eating healthy food and drinking plenty of water. When I was videoed, I look shattered but my message was good.

- On Saturday night we had Leila's birthday party with her friends.

- On Sunday morning I had just dropped Kerry off to his late parents' new apartment and got back into my car ready to drive home and catch up on sleep when Leila called and said, "Don't worry, Mum, I'm not hurt, but I've had a car accident." It was a relief she was okay!

I was pleased I had survived my week of challenges. I think I was still sane!

A year later, after being in hospital for four-and-a-half years, my father passed away. We had rushed to his bedside a few times, however, this time I was speaking at a National Speakers promotion night. I had organized to collect the girls and leave straight after my presentation to visit the hospital. I called at six and Mum told me he had just passed away while they were having a drink and a sing song with him.

My mind went into scramble mode as I was scheduled for my presentation in twenty minutes. I felt I needed to live up to Dad's expectation and decided to go ahead. I had some arnica and rescue remedy with me and in a quiet room swallowed all I had and worked on getting my head into the right space. Before I went on stage I told the emcee and asked him to rescue me if I fell to pieces. I couldn't tell anyone else as I thought I might break down in tears. I dedicated my presentation to Dad. It wasn't until I saw the DVD weeks later that I was surprised at how well I did. It was the hardest presentation in my life. I think Dad would have been proud of me.

Mum insisted that our father should come home for a few hours prior to the funeral as he hadn't been home since being admitted to the hospital. All the family was there and when the grandchildren were getting upset, Mum insisted that we all did the bird dance around him just before he left the house for his final time. It was one of his signature songs that he'd heard in Europe years ago. He played it at eight o'clock in the morning to get everyone out of bed to go boating and always had it ready at a party. The funeral director said it was the most unusual time he had ever seen that song played. Normally it's a party song, he said but as mum said, we were celebrating Dad's life.

When Dad had turned seventy, our family gave him a new organ for his birthday, which I now have in an upstairs room. It is very different playing the organ compared to the honky tonk of a piano, which I enjoy. Not long after he had passed away, I was re-learning to play one of his favorites Danny Boy. I was having a challenge and after I finished it, I immediately thought, "That was bloody awful!" I had learned we were all connected and certainly felt that Dad's spirit had been listening and let me know, I definitely needed more practice.

Once, after playing a few songs I had wandered downstairs to prepare dinner. A few minutes later Kerry said, "I thought you were upstairs. I can hear the organ still playing." I wasn't and assume Dad's spirit had come and had a 'wee tinkle on the ivories,' as we called it. Since his passing away, many times I have felt his presence around me, which is comforting and interesting.

Another time I was walking along the beach and had this huge sense of being lifted and carried along the beach with a message to 'hurry up and get on with your work.' It felt like big, soft angel wings and I sensed that meant my life story rather than the present work and business I was focusing on. Albeit my story needed to become the metaphor for my work as I focused and aligned to my life purpose.

A different experience was when I was walking along the beach and the old-fashioned yacht, *The Spirit of Adventure,* was moored in the bay. I had this huge sense that I had walking over and around me a lady in pioneering clothes, with a long dark skirt, long sleeved white blouse tucked into her skirt and an old fashioned dark pink bonnet on her head. It was Quaker style with the flat piece at the back and then an encasement around her hair with pleated frills around her face. She was looking at the boat and told me she was waiting for her fiancée, to arrive. Although I was used to the unusual experience this was another first time experience!

About this time "The Secret" was the latest personal development phenomenon on the market. I visited a friend to watch it. As I finished I had a split second vision of a red car with humps. I wasn't sure what it meant. I thought either a sponsor for the Self-Esteem Day or a car that I would own or influence my life in the future. I have searched for it and the closest I can find is a Morgan, Classic style MG or a Ferrari. Interesting again!

Both Kerry and I have seen black objects whizz past us in the house and have heard a squeaking noise, which when we went and checked was the rocking chair. No one else was in the house. He thought it was his mother.

I've had a few weird experiences with different birds. I was speaking on a cruise and invited mum to accompany me. We went to visit mum to invite her. We were sitting on the balcony when a paradise duck visited. It flew along the road then almost lost control of its wings as it maneuvered a ninety-degree turn and whizzed into the driveway. It dropped heavily onto the concrete and proceeded to waddle up the driveway. We watched in amazement. Mum said nothing like this had ever happened in twenty years. We joked that it was Dad visiting us to have a drink. She gave it some water which it devoured quickly and then circled my car three or four times pecking at the wheels.

Sometime later, I went and gave it more water. The duck seemed tame as it allowed me to walk within a few feet of it. Jokingly I asked the duck if it was Dad. I don't know what I expected for an answer, but the question seemed sensible at the time. It stood up and in the same uncontrolled fashion, like the flying and landing, it flapped one of its wings. I was really surprised but still thought it all a coincident. While we had dinner the duck curled up on the front doormat and slept. We couldn't find it when we left that night. It had must have stayed as it left its calling sign, by excreting on the front mat in the morning for Mum to clean up. It was a weird experience! It was incredible, one part of us thinking maybe this was Dad's spirit returning to visit us and the other part of us thinking this is crazy.

When I mentioned it my friend, Reverend Rhonda, she was adamant it was my father, and she said, "The universe is all connected."

Up until the end of 2009, I was trying to financially support myself so I could work on creating my messages. Finally, now that my financial world hit rock bottom with the recession and consequent business semi-collapsing I am turning this around. The only decision I know for sure is to follow the messages and guidance from above. I have to trust and have faith that if mankind needs this story, then with help and advice from others, my life story and some of its unusual events will become a vehicle to teach and help others.

And as I sit on the cliff top on a beautiful summer's day, I think that with all the religions in the world, all the chaos and love that somehow these messages I have received will make a difference to others and help them towards happiness and inner peace. In hindsight, it now appears that is the intention behind everything that has happened and now is time to share. It will make a difference to someone and save a life somewhere.

Many years ago my friend wanted to mail me a copy of her new book. I told her I had a sense something had to be written in the front of it, so I would visit her and collect it. I didn't know what my intuition was telling me, and her intuition told her we should sit and watch a video, this quote was the answer:

There is only one religion, the religion of Love,
There is only one language, the language of the Heart,
There is only one caste, the caste of Humanity,
There is only one law, the law of Karma,
There is only one God, He is Omnipresent.

—Sai Baba

AMEN

Hindsight Insight

In my role as a Success Coach, I use six areas in life to assess.

- Self/Me – As we 'become' ourselves
- Health/Wellbeing – Our bodies need to be healthy
- Relationships/Love – To love and be loved
- Career/Work/Business – Following our passion and purpose
- Financial/Security – Providing support and individual security
- Spiritual/Community – Being in touch with 'the Universe' God or helping the others

When creating happiness and success in our life, we need to assess each area of life. The best way is to rate them from one (low) to ten (high). The higher rated areas are where you have created happiness and success and the lower rated areas are where you still need to focus goals.

Which area of life are you successful in? Which areas do you need to focus your goals on?

_____

_____

_____

_____

_____

_____

In finding happiness and success you have free will to choose to become the best you wish your life. Your journey is to overcome challenges to fine-tune your life until you have created your heaven on earth. Often, your biggest challenge is where you will find the most lessons and possibly your life purpose and mission. Each person is unique with a special gift to offer the world.

How much on track are you to finding success and happiness? What is your biggest challenge and have you overcome it? OR, are you on track with your life purpose? The world is waiting for your input.

_____

_____

_____

_____

_____

_____

About the Author

Janice – works as a professional motivational speaker, business trainer and success coach motivating and inspiring people's thinking and attitude to springboard them to success. She's an expert, she says, because she had to do it for herself by understanding the thoughts that make the world her oyster!

Her greatest journey, after many stumbles along the way, was discovering her real self, re-aligning her dreams, creating them and then crossing them off her 'wish' list.

She calls herself the Attitude Specialist and works with training and at conferences for corporates, business groups and individuals, steering them towards empowerment and success. She has featured in magazines, radio, television, and growing internationally via the internet.

She is adamant that self-esteem is the key to success and shares a little of her knowledge in this book. She is the founder of the awareness day, Selfday International Self Esteem Day and helps thousands worldwide.

She writes and teaches others to become their best by aligning to their talents, gifts, greatness, and life purpose whilst overcoming their fear as they find happiness, success and love in life.

Always out of her comfort zone, her newest ventures include creating an online business with her products along with making a movie and a goal is to appear on with Oprah. She reads the same book as me, 'Daily Word from Unity' with our daily quotes and might want to discuss them, says Janice...or something else!

A personal message from Janice Davies
The lady with nice in her name

Life is a journey and every experience is an opportunity to learn in the 'school of life'.

In my journey, I have encountered some unusual situations which spurred me on to understand them. Not part of my goals I finally accept a greater force has been preparing me to embrace my life mission... teaching self esteem. I have founded Selfday – International Self Esteem Day and will expand this message globally in my movie.

It has taken me a few years to align myself and dying in October 2010 and being revived finally was my clincher to have faith in myself and 'the universe'.

The hindsight's insights in the book are opportunities for you to reassess your unique life journey and help align you to your life mission. I believe this is to become your best and in doing so, share your special gifts and talents with the world to help others and make the world a better place.

Best wishes

Janice – Queen of Self Esteem. www.internationalselfesteem.com

Other Books written by Janice

Sailing a Different Course

Say Yes to a Positive Attitude

200 PowerTips to Keep your Attitude Positive

How to Achieve your Dream Life

Be A Winner and Believe in Yourself

Dealing with Difficult People and Tricky Situations

DVD's

Your Guide to True Happiness

How to Deal with Toxic Employees

Revamp Yourself

Online Courses

Attitude Training For You

www.attitudetrainingforyou.com

Self Esteem Academy – Daily Self Esteem Ideas

www.selfesteemday.com

Dealing with Difficult People & Tricky Situations

www.difficultpeoplehelp.com

XFactor Confidence – 3 Vital Keys to Create More Success and More Money

www.xfactorconfidence.com

Think Positive to Be A Success – Boost Your Attitude to A+

www.thinkpositivetobeasuccess.com

Order Form

Copy or Scan this Form for more information or orders

Telephone: + 64 09 424 8400

Email: janice@attitudespecialist.co.nz

Postal: P O Box 83218 Edmonton Auckland New Zealand 0652

Please send the following books, DVD or reports. I understand that I may return them for a refund, within 30 days if in original condition.

Please check prices online to Pay ONLINE VIA PAYPAL before order is posted. Postage will be added to product price.

_____

_____

_____

_____

_____

Please send more free information

☐ on: Other Books

☐ Speaking/Seminars

☐ Coaching

☐ In-House Training

Name of Products: _____

_____

_____

_____

_____

_____

_____

Your Name: _____

Address: _____

_____

Email Address:_____

Contact Information

Janice Davies

Attitude Specialist

P O Box 83218 Edmonton Auckland, New Zealand

Mobile: +64 021 514 511

Phone: 09 424 8400 (International +64 9424 8400)

Email: janice@attitudespecialist.com

www.attitudespecialst.com

Visit us for book information and links to our other sister sites.

Check our websites for news, book updates, resources and more or to register to receive:

- Free weekly Motivational Quotes,
- Attitude Ezine

Read our regular articles on our blog:

www.attitudespecialst.blogspot.com

Follow the Attitude Specialist on:

- Twitter - www.twitter.com/AttitudeTrainer
- You Tube - www.youtube.com/janicemaydavies
- Facebook - www.facebook.com/JaniceDaviesGuru

Contact us on SKYPE – Janice Davies – attitudespecialist

FREE

LIFELONG MEMBERSHIP

ATTITUDE ACHIEVERS Club

Come and join our free membership program when you will receive upon registration;

- Free Success Attitude Webinar
- Free 5 day Success Coaching E-Course
- Free MPS interview
- Free 5 day Self Esteem E-Course
- Free Success Journal
- Free Poems:

  Attitude Poem – Charles Swindoll
  Our Greatest Fear – Marianne Williamson
  (made famous by Nelson Mandela)

- Free weekly motivational quote
- Free weekly video Attitude PowerTip
- Exclusive membership offers

Visit this link to register –
http://www.thesuccessattitude.info

www.ingramcontent.com/pod-product-compliance
Lightning Source LLC
Chambersburg PA
CBHW030012110426
42741CB00032B/403